THE MEDICO-LEGAL CASES OF INDIA

A QUICK REFERENCE COMPENDIUM FOR MEDICO-LEGAL CASES IN INDIA

DR. NITIN TABIB

Made with ♥ on the Notion Press Platform

www.notionpress.com

To

The most amazing sister in the world

Dr. Gowri Joshi

The younger sibling who is often like the elder one.

Contents

Preface

This book began not in a courtroom or a classroom, but in the space between them - a space I have occupied, in one form or another, for most of my working life.

My career has moved through more disciplines than most: a management education at Jamnalal Bajaj Institute of Management Studies, three decades in corporate India including Siemens, IBM, and EY - largely in sales and business development, where I learned that every deal, every client relationship, and every escalation eventually comes down to risk, trust, and the fine print nobody reads until something goes wrong. Somewhere along the way, that curiosity about risk pulled me toward the law, and I completed my LLB from the University of Mumbai. I already had a doctorate in management and was UGC-NET qualified, and today I teach as an Associate Professor at DMTIMS, where I sit, every day, at the intersection of management thinking and the next generation of professionals who will run businesses, advise clients, and make decisions that affect real lives.

I am also a partner at MedLex360 LLP, an emerging medico-legal consulting firm in India. Based on my interactions in this capacity with various people, I found, repeatedly, that doctors, hospital administrators, lawyers, and management students were all circling the same handful of Supreme Court and NCDRC judgments, but from entirely different directions and with entirely different vocabularies. A clinician would ask what a judgment meant for their consent form. A law student would ask what standard of proof it demanded. A hospital administrator would ask what it meant for their SOPs and their liability insurance. A management student, trained to think in terms of process, governance, and risk, would ask an equally valid but differently framed question: what did this organisation fail to build, and how do you build it so this doesn't happen again? I realised that no single existing resource spoke to all four audiences in the same language, using the same set of facts.

And thus, the idea for this book shaped up - my earnest attempt to close that gap.

For doctors and healthcare professionals, this compendium translates dense legal judgments into plain, clinically relevant lessons - what went wrong, what the court expected instead, and what documentation or communication would have changed the outcome. It is meant to be read not as case law, but as a risk-management manual grounded in real judgments rather than hypotheticals.

For lawyers and law students, each case is presented with the full apparatus of legal analysis - citation, issues, arguments on both sides, ratio decidendi, and significance - so that this can serve as a genuine quick-reference companion for practice before consumer fora and civil courts, and as a structured introduction to medical negligence jurisprudence for those still in law school.

The QR Code provided with each case links to the authentic judgment copy taken from relevant official sources and put in a single data repository for your convenience. You may validate these using the citations provided. Please note that the QR codes are valid and working at the time of publishing this book. However, they may cease to function in the future in case of change in the URLs.

For hospital administrators and management professionals, my own background makes this, perhaps, the most personal section of the book. Every judgment discussed here is, underneath the legal language, a case study in organisational failure or organisational resilience - in documentation systems, escalation protocols, informed-consent processes, and the vicarious liability that follows when systems break down. I have tried to draw out the governance and risk-management lessons explicitly, because these cases are as relevant to a hospital's board and compliance function as they are to its treating physicians.

For students across all three disciplines, the book is designed to work as a reference book: each chapter is self-contained, standardised in structure, and followed by practice pearls and a documentation checklist that can anchor classroom discussion or case-based learning.

I do not think of this book as a legal treatise, nor as a medical manual, nor as a management case-study collection - though it borrows honestly from all three. I think of it as a shared reference point: a place where a doctor, a lawyer, a hospital administrator, and a student can look at the same case and walk away with a lesson relevant to their own vantage point.

I hope it serves that purpose for you.

- Dr. Nitin Tabib

DISCLAIMER:

This compendium is compiled for reference and educational purposes only. While every effort has been made to ensure accuracy, readers are advised to verify citations and refer to original judgments before reliance in legal proceedings. The annotations and summaries herein represent an editorial synthesis and do not constitute legal advice.

Acknowledgments

No meaningful work is ever truly the product of one individual. This book is no exception.

My journey into the study of law began during my time at law school, where I was introduced to the intellectual rigor, analytical discipline, and enduring relevance of legal principles. The education I received there not only shaped my understanding of the law but also instilled a lifelong curiosity about the intersection of legal doctrine and professional practice. I remain deeply grateful to my teachers and mentors whose guidance sparked and nurtured that interest.

This book owes much to my friends in the medical profession. Through countless conversations with clinicians, surgeons, and healthcare professionals, I was introduced to the fascinating and often misunderstood world of medico-legal practice. Their experiences highlighted the growing importance of legal awareness in healthcare and inspired the idea of creating a practical resource that bridges the gap between medicine and law.

I would like to express my special gratitude to K. Sreekala Appunni, a dear academic friend and topper of LLB at University of Mumbai (Class of 2026), for her invaluable assistance in reviewing and validating the legal and factual aspects of the cases discussed in this book. Her thoughtful insights, attention to detail, and willingness to engage in rigorous discussions greatly helped to enhance the accuracy and reliability of this compilation. Any errors that remain are, of course, entirely my own.

I must also acknowledge the remarkable role of modern technology and artificial intelligence in the creation of this work. The ability to efficiently access, organize, compare, and synthesize large volumes of legal material has transformed the process of legal research and writing. Tools powered by artificial intelligence enabled me to assemble, verify, structure, and refine this compilation in ways that would have been unimaginable only a few years ago. While technology can never replace human judgment, it has become an invaluable partner in scholarship and knowledge creation.

Finally, I would like to thank all the judges, lawyers, doctors, patients, and healthcare institutions whose experiences have contributed to the development of Indian medico-legal jurisprudence. Every case discussed in this book represents real people, real challenges, and important lessons. It is through their stories that the law continues to evolve and improve the standards of healthcare and patient protection in our country.

I hope this book serves as a useful guide for medical professionals, students, administrators, legal practitioners, and anyone interested in understanding the evolving relationship between medicine and the law.

- Dr. Nitin Tabib

Prologue/Introduction

Overview

Medical law in India operates at the intersection of several legal regimes: the Law of Torts (civil liability for negligence), the Indian Penal Code (criminal liability under Section 304A for death by negligence), the Consumer Protection Act 1986/2019 (consumer rights in healthcare), the Indian Medical Council Act (professional misconduct), and constitutional provisions (right to health as part of the right to life under Article 21).

The Consumer Protection Act and Healthcare

The landmark Supreme Court judgment in Indian Medical Association v. V.P. Shantha (1995) 6 SCC 651 held that medical services fall within the ambit of 'service' under the Consumer Protection Act, 1986. This opened a new and accessible avenue for patients to seek redress through consumer fora at the district, state, and national levels, in addition to civil courts and criminal proceedings. The Consumer Protection Act, 2019 has since updated the framework with enhanced penalties, a mediation mechanism, and enhanced pecuniary jurisdictions.

The Standard of Care: The Bolam and Bolitho Tests

Indian courts have consistently applied the Bolam test (derived from the English case Bolam v. Friern Hospital Management Committee [1957]) as the primary measure of the standard of care expected from medical professionals. Under this test, a doctor is not negligent if the treatment accorded with a practice accepted by a responsible body of medical opinion, even if another responsible body would have acted differently. However, in cases such as Arun Kumar Manglik v. Chirayu Health (2019), the Supreme Court has introduced the Bolitho qualification - that the practice defended must itself be logically defensible, not merely common.

Criminal vs. Civil Negligence

The Supreme Court in Jacob Mathew v. State of Punjab (2005) drew a clear line between civil negligence (attracting compensation liability) and criminal negligence (attracting prosecution under Section 304A IPC). Criminal negligence requires that the conduct be grossly negligent - so reckless as to show disregard for human life - whereas civil negligence requires only a departure from the standard of a reasonably competent practitioner.

Vicarious Liability of Hospitals

Hospitals in India are held vicariously liable for the negligent acts of their employed doctors, and increasingly for the acts of consulting and contractual doctors, as established in Pooja Sharma v. Maharaja Agrasen Hospital (2019) and the line of cases following Indian Medical Association v. V.P. Shantha. The Consumer Protection Act provides an accessible mechanism for such claims.

Informed Consent

The right to informed consent in India received its most authoritative judicial articulation in Samira Kohli v. Dr. Prabha Manchanda (2008). Consent must be specific to each procedure, must be given by a competent adult patient personally, and must be preceded by adequate disclosure of risks and alternatives. Emergency exceptions exist only in genuine life-threatening situations.

Compensation Principles

The Supreme Court has evolved a comprchensive framework for computing compensation in medical negligence cases, particularly in cases involving death or permanent disability. Key factors include the victim's income and earning potential, medical expenses (past and future), pain and suffering, loss of consortium, and the nature and permanence of the injury. Balram Prasad v.

Kunal Saha (2013) remains the high-water mark for compensation quantum in Indian medical negligence law.

What this compendium offers

This compendium brings together a few medico-legal judgments delivered by the Supreme Court of India and the National Consumer Disputes Redressal Commission (NCDRC). The cases selected represent the most frequently cited, most doctrinally significant, and most practically impactful decisions in the field of medical negligence and patient rights in India. Also included are some landmark judgments that have paved the way for medico-legal realm.

The interface between medicine and law in India has grown enormously complex over the past two decades. The Consumer Protection Act, 1986 opened the doors of consumer fora to patients seeking redress for medical negligence, transforming healthcare from a purely professional relationship to one with defined consumer rights. Simultaneously, criminal liability under Section 304A of the Indian Penal Code continued to be invoked - sometimes appropriately, sometimes frivolously - requiring the courts to repeatedly draw and redraw the line between an unfortunate medical outcome and culpable negligence.

The cases in this compendium are drawn from across various parts of India - West Bengal, Delhi, Maharashtra, Andhra Pradesh, Punjab, Kerala, and Madhya Pradesh - reflecting the pan-national character of the legal developments. They span civil, criminal, and consumer protection proceedings, providing a multi-dimensional view of the legal landscape.

Each case is presented in a standardised format comprising: the full case name and citation, the court and date of judgment, the background facts, the issues raised, arguments of both parties, the ruling, key legal principles, the outcome, and the case's broader significance. This structure is designed to serve as a quick-reference tool for lawyers and doctors alike.

A QR code is provided with each case that links to the judgment copy. For your convenience, all judgments are downloaded from various official sources and uploaded on cloud for ease of access. You may validate these at your own free will should you so desire.

This compendium is intended for use by advocates practising in consumer fora and civil courts, medical practitioners seeking to understand their legal exposure, hospital administrators developing compliance frameworks, medical students and law students engaged in academic study, and forensic medicine practitioners involved in medico-legal investigations.

Why Every Doctor Should Know These Cases

Most doctors never imagine that one day they will find themselves sitting across a lawyer, reading a legal notice, answering questions before a committee, or defending a decision made in an operating theatre, ICU, OPD, or emergency room.

Yet it happens.

Not because doctors stop caring.

Not because every adverse outcome is negligence.

But because medicine today exists in a world where every clinical decision is scrutinised, documented, questioned, and sometimes litigated.

A patient may forget the medicine prescribed. They may not remember the dosage. They may not even recall the exact diagnosis.

But they rarely forget how they felt when something went wrong.

That is where medico-legal cases begin.

A medico-legal case is not merely a dispute between a doctor and a patient. It is a collision between medicine and law. One profession seeks to heal; the other seeks accountability. When these worlds intersect, courts are often called upon to determine whether a doctor acted with reasonable skill, care, and diligence.

For many practitioners, the legal system appears intimidating. Legal terminology, courtroom procedures, consumer complaints, police investigations, medical councils, expert opinions, compensation claims - these are not subjects taught extensively in medical school. Most doctors spend years learning anatomy, pathology, pharmacology, and surgery, but very little time learning how courts evaluate their actions.

This knowledge gap can be costly.

The reality is that a significant number of medico-legal disputes do not arise because a doctor lacked clinical competence. They arise because of poor documentation, inadequate communication, improper consent, missing records, unrealistic expectations, delayed referrals, or failure to follow established protocols.

A technically sound treatment can become legally vulnerable if it is poorly documented.

Conversely, even in difficult clinical situations with unfavourable outcomes, a doctor who communicates effectively, maintains accurate records, obtains informed consent, and follows accepted standards of care is often in a far stronger legal position.

Understanding medico-legal principles is therefore no longer optional. It has become an essential component of modern medical practice.

Medicine Is Not an Exact Science

One of the greatest misconceptions held by the public is that medicine guarantees outcomes.

It does not.

Medicine is a science of probabilities, not certainties.

Two patients with the same diagnosis may respond differently to identical treatment. A surgery performed flawlessly may still result in complications. A rare adverse drug reaction can occur despite all precautions. A patient may deteriorate despite the best efforts of an experienced medical team.

The law recognises this reality.

Indian courts have repeatedly emphasised that a doctor is not an insurer of success. The mere fact that treatment failed or a patient suffered an adverse outcome does not automatically mean negligence.

The legal question is different.

The question is not: "Did the patient survive?"

The question is: "Did the doctor act in a manner that a reasonably competent medical professional would have acted under similar circumstances?"

That distinction lies at the heart of medical negligence law.

The Changing Doctor-Patient Relationship

For generations, medical practice in India operated largely on trust.

- A doctor advised
- A patient complied
- Questions were limited
- Records were brief
- Consent forms were often treated as formalities

Those days have changed.

Today's patients are informed, connected, and empowered. They seek second opinions, conduct online research, access medical literature, compare treatment options, and are increasingly aware of their legal rights.

This transformation is neither good nor bad.

It is simply the new reality.

The modern doctor must therefore be both: **a clinician and a communicator.**

Patients are far less likely to challenge a doctor who explains clearly, listens patiently, documents thoroughly, and demonstrates empathy.

Many medico-legal disputes begin not with negligence, but with dissatisfaction.

And dissatisfaction often begins with poor communication.

Civil Liability, Criminal Liability, and Consumer Complaints

One of the most common fears among doctors is the possibility of legal action. However, not all legal proceedings are the same.

A patient may file a complaint before a Consumer Commission seeking compensation.

A civil suit may be instituted for damages.

In rare situations involving allegations of gross negligence, criminal proceedings may be initiated.

Each process has different standards, different consequences, and different legal thresholds. Importantly, Indian courts have consistently recognised that criminal prosecution of doctors should be reserved for exceptional cases involving gross or reckless negligence - not merely an error of judgment or an unfortunate outcome. Understanding this distinction can help doctors respond rationally rather than emotionally when faced with legal scrutiny.

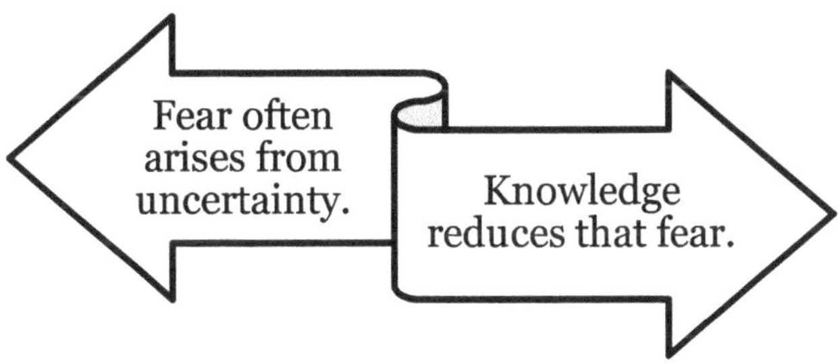

The Three Pillars of Medico-Legal Protection

After studying hundreds of medico-legal disputes across India, certain patterns emerge repeatedly.

Regardless of speciality, hospital size, or geographic location, three factors consistently influence legal outcomes.

1. **Communication**
   Patients are generally more forgiving of complications than they are of silence. Clear explanations build trust while unanswered questions create suspicion.

2. **Documentation**
   Courts decide cases on evidence. And in medical practice, records are evidence. If it is not documented, it becomes difficult to prove that it happened.
   Detailed notes, treatment records, consent forms, referral advice, investigation reports, discharge summaries, and follow-up instructions can often become a doctor's strongest defence.

3. **Consent**
   Consent is far more than a signature. True informed consent requires discussion. Patients should understand the proposed treatment, its benefits, risks, alternatives, and possible consequences.

Many landmark judgments included in this book arose because consent was either inadequate or improperly obtained.

Why This Book Was Written

Doctors are frequently told to "be careful." But rarely are they shown exactly what courts have said, why certain doctors were held liable, why others were exonerated, and what practical lessons can be learned from those decisions.

This book attempts to bridge that gap. It does not seek to criticise doctors. Nor does it seek to encourage defensive medicine. Its purpose is informational - and to some extent - educational.

The cases included in these pages represent some of the most influential medico-legal decisions delivered by Indian courts and tribunals. Together, they have shaped the legal principles that govern medical practice today.

Some judgments strengthened patient rights.
Others protected doctors from unfair prosecution.

Many clarified important questions relating to consent, negligence, compensation, documentation, criminal liability, expert evidence, and hospital responsibility.

Each case tells a story.

Behind every judgment lies a patient, a family, a doctor, a difficult clinical decision, and a legal question that required resolution.

The objective is not merely to understand the law.
The objective is to learn from it.

A Final Word

Medicine remains one of the noblest professions. Every day, doctors make decisions under pressure, often with incomplete information, limited time, and enormous responsibility.

The law does not expect perfection.

It expects reasonableness.

It does not demand guaranteed outcomes.

It demands reasonable care.

The judgments discussed in this book remind us that good medicine and good medico-legal practice are not opposing concepts. They are partners.

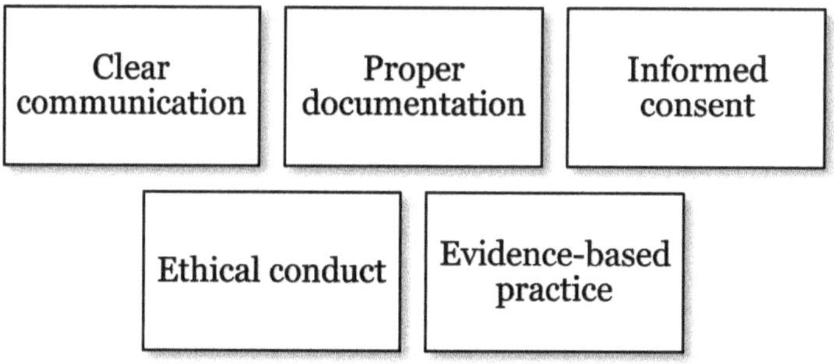

These principles not only improve patient care; they also provide the strongest shield against medico-legal disputes.

If this book helps even one doctor avoid a preventable medico-legal problem, improve documentation, strengthen communication with patients, or better understand the legal principles governing medical practice, it will have achieved its purpose.

- Dr. Nitin Tabib

A Quick Look

Sr.	Case	Year	Type	Core Principle
1	V.P. Shantha	1995	Consumer Protection	Medical services covered under Consumer Protection Act
2	Mr. X v. Hospital Z	1998	Privacy / Confidentiality	Confidentiality not absolute; disclosure permitted in exceptional circumstances
3	Vinitha Ashok	2001	Consumer Protection	Standard of care in pregnancy
4	Pravat Kumar Mukherjee	2005	Consumer Protection	Duty to provide emergency treatment regardless of payment
5	Jacob Mathew	2005	Criminal	Gross negligence required for criminal prosecution of doctors
6	Samira Kohli	2008	Consumer Protection	Informed consent and patient autonomy
7	Malay Kumar Ganguly	2009	Civil & Criminal	Gross negligence and standards of expert evidence
8	Nizam's Institute	2009	Consumer Protection	Compensation principles for permanent disability
9	Martin F. D'Souza	2009	Consumer Protection	Expert opinion in medical negligence cases

Sr.	Case	Year	Type	Core Principle
10	Nikhil Super Speciality Hospital	2010	Consumer Protection	Expert evidence not mandatory in every case
11	Kusum Sharma v. Batra Hospital	2010	Consumer Protection	Comprehensive principles governing medical negligence
12	Balram Prasad	2013	Consumer Protection	Record compensation in medical negligence
13	Maharaja Agrasen Hospital	2019	Consumer Protection	Hospital vicarious liability and guideline-based care
14	Shiv Ram	2005	Civil	Res ipsa loquitur does not apply to sterilisation failure; natural causes (e.g. spontaneous recanalisation) do not imply negligence
15	Asha Jaiswal	2021	Consumer Protection	Res ipsa loquitur in medical negligence
16	Smt. Santra	2000	Civil	Failed sterilisation and wrongful conception
17	Achutrao Haribhau Khodwa	1996	Civil	Foreign object left in body; res ipsa loquitur
18	Spring Meadows Hospital	1998	Consumer Protection	Hospital liability and compensation for catastrophic injury
19	Savita Garg	2004	Consumer Protection	Burden of producing medical records

Sr.	Case	Year	Type	Core Principle
20	Jaspal Singh	2009	Consumer Protection	Retained surgical instrument and systems failure
21	Dr. Harish Kumar Khurana	2021	Consumer Protection	Surgical complications vs negligence; importance of expert evidence
22	Dr. Archana Sharma	2022	Criminal Law Reform	Misuse of criminal process against doctors
23	Dr. Suresh Gupta v. Govt. of NCT Delhi	2004	Criminal	Distinction between civil and criminal negligence
24	Parmanand Katara	1989	Constitutional / PIL	Duty to provide emergency care
25	Common Cause Case	2018	Constitutional	Living wills and passive euthanasia
26	Aruna Shanbaug	2011	Constitutional	Judicial recognition of passive euthanasia
27	Savelife Foundation (Good Samaritan Law)	2016	Constitutional / PIL	Legal protection for bystanders and Good Samaritans assisting accident victims
28	M.A. Biviji	2023	Consumer Protection / Medical Negligence	Higher evidentiary burden for medical negligence; adverse outcome alone does not prove breach of duty
29	V. Krishnakumar (Retinopathy of Prematurity)	2015	Consumer Protection	Failure to advise mandatory ROP screening in a high-risk neonate constitutes negligence

Sr.	Case	Year	Type	Core Principle
30	Cetty Koteswara Rao	2026	Consumer Protection	Burden of proof lies on complainant; adverse outcome alone does not establish negligence
31	Poonam Verma (Cross-Pathy: Negligence Per Se)	1996	Civil / Consumer Protection	Practicing outside one's registered system of medicine is negligence per se
32	Paschim Banga Khet Mazdoor Samiti	1996	Constitutional	Right to emergency medical care is part of the right to life under Article 21
33	Arun Kumar Manglik	2019	Consumer Protection	Published clinical guidelines (WHO/NVBDCP) define the standard of care; Bolitho refinement applied
34	Dr. Jayshree Ujwal Ingole	2017	Criminal	Criminal liability attaches only to grossly negligent or reckless medical conduct

DEAR READER,
At the end of every chapter,
you will find a section called
"MEDLEX360 PRACTICE PEARLS"
This section contains the
MAIN TAKEAWAY
from the case, along with
practical risk management tips
and a documentation checklist.
PLEASE READ IT CAREFULLY.
LEGAL ADVISOR
THE LAW FAVOURS THE PREPARED.
Good knowledge today can protect you
and your patients tomorrow.

1. V.P. Shantha

Full Case Name	Indian Medical Association v. V.P. Shantha & Ors.
Citation / Case Number	(1995) 6 SCC 651 | AIR 1996 SC 550
Court / Forum	Supreme Court of India
Date of Judgment	13 November 1995
State / Jurisdiction	Pan-India
Type of Case	Consumer Protection

Background & Facts

Prior to this judgment, there was considerable uncertainty regarding whether medical practitioners and hospitals could be proceeded against under the Consumer Protection Act, 1986. Various High Courts and Consumer Fora had delivered conflicting decisions on whether medical services constituted a "service" within the meaning of Section 2(1)(o) of the Act.

A batch of appeals, writ petitions, and special leave petitions came before the Supreme Court raising a common question: whether services rendered by doctors, hospitals, nursing homes, and medical institutions fall within the scope of the Consumer Protection Act, thereby enabling patients to seek redress before Consumer Fora for medical negligence and deficiency in service.

Issues Raised

- Whether medical services rendered by doctors and hospitals constitute "service" under Section 2(1)(o) of the Consumer Protection Act, 1986.
- Whether patients receiving medical treatment are "consumers" under the Act.

- Whether government hospitals and charitable hospitals fall within the ambit of the Act.
- Whether free medical services are covered under the Consumer Protection Act.
- Whether the doctor-patient relationship is a "contract of service" or a "contract for services."

Arguments - Petitioners

The medical profession argued that medicine is a profession and not a commercial activity. It was contended that the doctor-patient relationship is based upon trust, skill, and professional judgment and should not be equated with ordinary commercial services. It was further argued that doctors are already regulated by Medical Councils and should not be subjected to consumer jurisdiction.

Arguments - Respondents

The respondents contended that patients pay consideration for medical treatment and therefore are consumers of healthcare services. They argued that patients who suffer injury due to negligence or deficiency in service should have access to a speedy, inexpensive, and effective remedy through Consumer Fora instead of lengthy civil litigations.

Judgment & Ruling

The Supreme Court held that medical services rendered for consideration fall within the definition of "service" under the Consumer Protection Act, 1986. Consequently, doctors, hospitals, and nursing homes providing paid medical treatment can be proceeded against before Consumer Fora for deficiency in service. The Court rejected the argument that the medical profession enjoys immunity merely because it is a profession.

The Court distinguished between a "contract of personal service" (master-servant relationship), which is excluded from the Act, and a "contract for services" (professional engagement), which is covered. The doctor-patient relationship was held to be a contract for services.

Key Holdings:

- **Medical services are "services" under the Consumer Protection Act:** Except if provided entirely free of charge.
- **Doctors and hospitals are liable:** They can be held accountable for deficiency in service and medical negligence.
- **Completely free treatment is excluded:** Patients receiving wholly free treatment are not consumers under the Act.
- **Mixed-payment hospitals are covered:** hospitals that treat some patients free of charge while charging others are covered, and even the free patients are entitled to invoke consumer jurisdiction because they are beneficiaries of the overall service arrangement.
- **Insurance/employer-paid treatment is covered:** Such treatment is not considered free service.
- **Medical practice is a "contract for service":** It is covered by the Act, unlike a contract of service.
- **Consumer forums can hear negligence claims:** They have jurisdiction over medical negligence complaints.
- **Consumer remedy is additional:** It supplements, not replaces, other legal remedies.

KEY LEGAL PRINCIPLES / RATIO DECIDENDI

- Medical services rendered for consideration constitute "service" under Section 2(1)(o) of the Consumer Protection Act, 1986.
- Patients receiving paid medical treatment are "consumers."
- The doctor-patient relationship is a contract for services, not a contract of personal service.
- Medical professionals do not enjoy immunity from consumer jurisdiction merely because medicine is a profession.
- Hospitals providing both paid and free treatment are covered under the Act.
- Beneficiaries of services paid for through insurance schemes, employer-sponsored healthcare, or similar arrangements are also consumers.
- Purely charitable institutions rendering treatment entirely free of charge fall outside the Consumer Protection Act.

Compensation / Outcome

The case did not involve an award of compensation. The Supreme Court resolved the legal issue and held that medical services rendered for consideration are amenable to the jurisdiction of Consumer Fora under the Consumer Protection Act, 1986.

Significance & Impact

This is arguably the most important medico-legal judgment in Indian healthcare jurisprudence. It fundamentally transformed the legal relationship between doctors and patients by recognising patients as consumers and healthcare providers as service providers under consumer law.

Virtually every major medical negligence case decided thereafter - including Jacob Mathew, Kusum Sharma, Samira Kohli, Nizam's Institute, Balram Prasad, and Maharaja Agrasen Hospital - rests upon the legal foundation established in this judgment. The decision opened the doors of Consumer Fora to medical negligence victims and remains the cornerstone of medical negligence litigation in India.

MEDLEX360 PRACTICE PEARLS	
What changed?	For the first time, doctors and hospitals providing paid treatment became answerable before Consumer Fora for deficiency in service.
Risk Management Takeaways	• Every patient is potentially a consumer. • Documentation is your first line of defence. • Communication failures frequently become legal disputes. • Hospitals must maintain robust consent and record-keeping systems. • Consumer complaints can arise even when treatment is clinically appropriate if communication is poor.
Documentation Checklist	• Complete medical records • Informed consent forms • Investigation reports • Discharge summaries • Follow-up instructions • Billing and treatment records

When healthcare became a consumer service, documentation became a legal necessity.

2. Mr. X v. Hospital Z

Full Case Name	Mr. X v. Hospital Z
Citation / Case Number	(1998) 8 SCC 296 | AIR 1999 SC 495 | Civil Appeal No. 4641 of 1998
Court / Forum	Supreme Court of India
Date of Judgment	21 September 1998
State / Jurisdiction	Pan-India
Type of Case	Medical Confidentiality / Right to Privacy / HIV Disclosure

Background & Facts

The appellant, referred to as Mr. X, was a medical doctor whose marriage had been arranged with a woman identified as Ms. Y. During medical testing conducted at the respondent hospital, Mr. X was found to be HIV-positive.

The hospital disclosed his HIV-positive status to persons connected with the proposed marriage. As a result, the marriage was cancelled. Thereafter, members of his family and community became aware of his condition, leading to social ostracism and significant personal hardship.

Mr. X approached the National Consumer Disputes Redressal Commission (NCDRC), alleging that the hospital had unlawfully disclosed confidential medical information and seeking compensation for breach of confidentiality. The NCDRC dismissed the complaint, after which he appealed to the Supreme Court.

Issues Raised

- Whether a hospital is under an absolute duty to maintain confidentiality regarding a patient's medical condition.

- Whether disclosure of a patient's HIV-positive status without consent amounts to a violation of the right to privacy under Article 21 of the Constitution.
- Whether disclosure is permissible when another identifiable person may be exposed to a serious health risk.
- Whether the prospective spouse has a right to know information that may directly affect her life and health.

Arguments - Appellant

- Medical confidentiality is a fundamental ethical and legal obligation.
- The hospital breached its duty of care by revealing confidential medical information without consent.
- The disclosure violated his constitutional right to privacy under Article 21.
- The cancellation of his marriage and subsequent social stigma resulted directly from the hospital's unlawful conduct.

Arguments - Respondents

- Confidentiality is not an absolute obligation.
- Disclosure was necessary to protect an identifiable person from a serious communicable disease.
- The prospective spouse had a legitimate right to be informed of a significant health risk.
- Public health considerations outweighed the patient's claim of confidentiality in the circumstances of the case.

Judgment & Ruling

The Supreme Court dismissed the appeal and upheld the hospital's action.

The Court held that although medical confidentiality and privacy are important legal rights, they are not absolute. Disclosure may be justified where non-disclosure would expose another identifiable person to a serious risk of harm.

The Court observed that the proposed marriage would have placed Ms. Y at risk of contracting a serious communicable disease. In such circumstances, the hospital's disclosure was justified in the interest of protecting her health and life.

The Court further held that where two fundamental rights come into conflict - Mr. X's right to privacy and Ms. Y's right to life and health - the right that better serves public interest and protection of life must prevail.

Accordingly, disclosure of the HIV-positive status did not amount to an actionable breach of confidentiality or privacy in the facts of the case.

Key Holdings:

- Medical confidentiality is **not absolute.**
- Disclosure of HIV status may be justified to protect another person's life or health.
- Right to privacy under Article 21 is not absolute and may yield to compelling public interest.
- A prospective spouse has a right to know if the other party is HIV-positive before marriage.
- Doctors are protected when disclosure is made in good faith to prevent harm.
- The hospital was not liable for disclosing the patient's HIV status in the circumstances.
- Public health concerns can outweigh confidentiality where there is a real risk of transmission.
- The judgment emphasised balancing privacy with the right to life of others.

KEY LEGAL PRINCIPLES / RATIO DECIDENDI

- The right to privacy under Article 21 is not absolute.
- Medical confidentiality may be overridden where disclosure is necessary to prevent serious harm to an identifiable person.
- Public health considerations may justify limited disclosure of confidential medical information.
- A prospective spouse has a legitimate interest in being informed of a serious communicable disease that may affect marital life and health.
- Courts may balance competing fundamental rights and prefer the right that better protects life, health, and public welfare.
- The duty of confidentiality is subject to exceptions recognised by medical ethics and public interest.

Compensation / Outcome

No compensation was awarded.

The Supreme Court dismissed the appeal and held that the hospital was justified in disclosing the appellant's HIV-positive status to prevent serious harm to the prospective spouse.

Significance & Impact

This is one of India's leading medico-legal decisions on confidentiality and privacy.

The judgment established that:

- Doctor-patient confidentiality is not absolute.
- Disclosure may be justified where public interest or protection of another person's life and health is involved.

- Courts will balance privacy rights against competing rights under Article 21.
- Healthcare professionals may disclose confidential information where a serious and identifiable risk exists to another person.

The case became a foundational precedent in discussions involving HIV disclosure, communicable diseases, medical ethics, confidentiality, and patient privacy in India

MEDLEX360 PRACTICE PEARLS	
What changed?	The case clarified that confidentiality is a rule, but not an absolute rule. Exceptions exist where non-disclosure may expose another person to serious danger.
Risk Management Takeaways	• Maintain confidentiality as the default position. • Disclose patient information only when legally justified. • Carefully document reasons for any disclosure. • Seek specialist legal or ethics advice in difficult cases. • Balance patient privacy against foreseeable harm to identifiable third parties.
Documentation Checklist	• HIV counselling records • Consent documentation • Risk communication notes • Ethical committee recommendations (where applicable) • Reasons supporting disclosure • Records of persons informed and circumstances of disclosure

Confidentiality protects patients, but the law may permit disclosure when silence would expose another person to a serious and foreseeable risk.

3. Vinitha Ashok

Full Case Name	Smt. Vinitha Ashok v. Lakshmi Hospital & Ors.
Citation / Case Number	Appeal (Civil) No. 2977 of 1992 | (2001) 8 SCC 731 | AIR 2001 SC 3914
Court / Forum	Supreme Court of India
Date of Judgment	25 September 2001
State / Jurisdiction	Kerala
Type of Case	Civil / Consumer Protection

Background & Facts

The appellant, Smt. Vinitha Ashok, was admitted to Lakshmi Hospital, Kerala, following symptoms of ectopic pregnancy. The hospital's medical staff performed a procedure that resulted in the removal of her uterus. The appellant contended that the removal of her uterus was performed negligently and without adequate informed consent. She filed a complaint before the National Consumer Disputes Redressal Commission (NCDRC) seeking compensation for the loss of her reproductive organ.

Issues Raised

Whether the removal of the uterus during treatment for ectopic pregnancy amounted to medical negligence. Whether the standard of care exercised by the treating doctors was in accordance with accepted medical practice.

Arguments - Complainant / Appellant

The appellant argued that the removal of her uterus was an act of medical negligence, that she was not properly informed of the possibility of such a drastic intervention, and that there was a failure of duty of care on the part of the hospital and its doctors.

Arguments - Respondent

The respondents contended that the surgical intervention was necessary given the clinical condition of the patient at the time, and that the procedure was performed in accordance with standard medical practice to save the patient's life.

Judgment & Ruling

The Supreme Court dismissed the appeal, holding that the appellant had failed to establish medical negligence on the part of the respondent hospital and doctors.

The Court found that the appellant suffered from a rare cervical ectopic pregnancy, which could not have been diagnosed through routine clinical examination at the relevant stage, and that the emergency hysterectomy was necessitated by life-threatening haemorrhage.

Applying the settled principles governing medical negligence, the Court observed that a doctor is not negligent merely because another course of treatment might have been adopted or because the treatment did not produce the desired outcome.

Since the respondents had acted in accordance with a practice accepted by a responsible body of medical professionals and exercised reasonable skill and care in the circumstances, no deficiency in service or negligence was established, and the dismissal of the compensation claim was affirmed.

Key Holdings:

- **Negligence must be affirmatively proved**; an adverse outcome alone does not establish negligence.
- **The Bolam test governs medical negligence:** A doctor is not negligent if the treatment accords with a responsible body of medical opinion.

- **Errors of judgment are not necessarily negligence** if the doctor exercised reasonable skill and care.
- **Hysterectomy was medically justified** to save the patient's life after uncontrollable bleeding.
- **Failure to perform an ultrasonogram was not negligent** because it would not have materially altered the diagnosis or treatment.
- **Courts should rely on credible expert medical evidence** when assessing allegations of negligence.
- **Medical decisions must be judged by the circumstances existing at the time of treatment,** not with hindsight.
- **The appeal was dismissed** as the appellant failed to establish medical negligence.

KEY LEGAL PRINCIPLES / RATIO DECIDENDI

➲ A doctor is not guilty of negligence if the treatment administered accords with a responsible body of medical opinion.

➲ The Bolam test (acting in accordance with accepted medical practice) is the relevant standard for assessing medical negligence in India.

➲ The burden of proof to establish medical negligence lies on the complainant.

➲ A mere difference in medical opinion or outcome does not constitute negligence.

Compensation / Outcome

The Supreme Court dismissed the appeal, finding no negligence on the part of the hospital or doctors. No compensation was awarded to the appellant.

Significance & Impact

This early post-Consumer Protection Act judgment reinforced the application of the Bolam test in Indian courts and clarified that adverse medical outcomes alone do not give rise to a finding of negligence. It established an important precedent that mere removal of an organ necessary to save a patient's life does not by itself constitute actionable negligence.

MEDLEX360 PRACTICE PEARLS	
What went wrong?	The patient alleged that a life-altering procedure was performed unnecessarily and without adequate explanation.
Risk Management Takeaways	• Explain why a major surgical decision becomes necessary during surgery. • Discuss foreseeable possibilities before obtaining consent • Document life-saving clinical decisions contemporaneously. • Record alternative options considered. • Maintain detailed operative notes.
Documentation Checklist	• Consent form • Operative findings • Intra-operative decision-making notes

When a surgery changes a patient's future, your documentation must explain why.

4. Pravat Kumar Mukherjee

Full Case Name	Pravat Kumar Mukherjee & Anr. v. Ruby General Hospital & Ors.
Citation / Case Number	Original Petition No. 90 of 2002 | II (2005) CPJ 35 (NC) | NCDRC
Court / Forum	National Consumer Disputes Redressal Commission (NCDRC), New Delhi
Date of Judgment	25 April 2005
State / Jurisdiction	West Bengal
Type of Case	Consumer Protection

Background & Facts

On 14 January 2001, Sumanta Mukherjee, a second-year B.Tech. student at Netaji Subhash Chandra Bose Engineering College, Kolkata, was injured when a bus belonging to the Calcutta Tramway Corporation collided with his motorbike. Sumanta was conscious and in possession of a valid mediclaim insurance policy of ₹ 65,000. He was taken to Ruby General Hospital, approximately one kilometre from the accident site. The hospital initially claimed it was not equipped to treat him and refused to commence treatment without obtaining an advance deposit, even though the patient had presented his mediclaim insurance certificate. After considerable delay and the insistence on advance payment, treatment began, but Sumanta succumbed to his injuries. His parents, the complainants, filed a complaint before the NCDRC alleging medical negligence, deficiency in service, and denial of emergency treatment.

Issues Raised

Whether the hospital's refusal to provide immediate emergency treatment to an accident victim who held a valid mediclaim policy, amounts to deficiency in service under the Consumer Protection Act, 1986. Whether a hospital can insist on advance payment before treating an emergency trauma patient.

Arguments - Complainant / Appellant

The complainants argued that the hospital denied emergency treatment to a conscious accident victim despite being the nearest medical facility and despite the patient holding a valid mediclaim policy. The delay in initiating treatment due to insistence on advance deposits directly contributed to the patient's death and constituted gross deficiency in service.

Arguments - Respondent

The hospital contended that it was not a trauma centre, that its facilities were limited, and that the delays in treatment were not the proximate cause of death. The hospital also argued that seeking advance deposits was standard administrative practice.

Judgment & Ruling

The NCDRC ruled in favour of the complainants, holding that the refusal to provide immediate emergency medical care to an accident victim constitutes gross deficiency in service under the Consumer Protection Act, 1986. The Commission held that any hospital, regardless of whether or not it is a designated trauma centre, is bound to provide first aid and stabilising care to an emergency patient. The insistence on advance deposit before treating an emergency case where the patient holds a valid mediclaim policy was held to be wholly unjustified and unconscionable.

Key Holdings:

- **Emergency treatment cannot be denied** for non-payment of advance fees.

- **Saving life takes priority over financial formalities.**
- **Hospitals owe a duty of immediate emergency care** to critically injured patients.
- **Withdrawal or refusal of treatment for non-payment amounts to deficiency in service.**
- **Consent requirements do not delay life-saving treatment** in emergencies.
- **Emergency patients are consumers** under the Consumer Protection Act, even if payment is deferred.
- **Compensation may include mental agony** caused by medical negligence.
- **Hospitals must prioritize medical ethics over commercial considerations.**

KEY LEGAL PRINCIPLES / RATIO DECIDENDI

- A hospital has a statutory and ethical duty to provide emergency treatment to accident victims and cannot withhold care pending payment of advance deposit.
- Possession of a valid mediclaim insurance policy by a patient removes the justification for any financial precondition to emergency treatment.
- Refusal or unreasonable delay in emergency treatment constitutes deficiency in service under the Consumer Protection Act, 1986.
- The nearest hospital to an accident site carries a special duty of care towards trauma victims.

Compensation / Outcome

The NCDRC awarded compensation to the complainant family, holding the hospital liable for deficiency in service. The Commission directed Ruby General Hospital to pay ₹ 1,10,000 as compensation, comprising ₹ 85,000 for medical expenses and loss, and ₹ 25,000 for pain and suffering.

Significance & Impact

This landmark NCDRC judgment played a seminal role in crystallising the legal obligation of hospitals to provide emergency treatment without demanding advance payments. It reinforced the right of patients to emergency medical care and is widely cited in subsequent consumer forum decisions involving denial of emergency treatment. It complemented the Supreme Court's earlier direction in Parmanand Katara v. Union of India regarding the duty of medical professionals to provide emergency care.

MEDLEX360 PRACTICE PEARLS	
What went wrong?	Emergency treatment was delayed because of administrative and payment-related issues.
Risk Management Takeaways	• Treat first, discuss payment later. • Never refuse emergency care because of financial formalities. • Stabilization is the first duty. • Train reception and billing staff regarding emergency protocols. • Maintain clear emergency triage policies.
Documentation Checklist	• Time of arrival • Initial assessment • Treatment initiated immediately

No hospital should allow billing procedures to stand between a patient and emergency care.

5. Jacob Mathew

Full Case Name	Jacob Mathew v. State of Punjab & Anr.
Citation / Case Number	Criminal Appeal Nos. 144-145 of 2004 | (2005) 6 SCC 1 | AIR 2005 SC 3180
Court / Forum	Supreme Court of India (Three-Judge Bench)
Date of Judgment	05 August 2005
State / Jurisdiction	Punjab
Type of Case	Criminal (Section 304A IPC)

Background & Facts

The appellant, Dr. Jacob Mathew, was a doctor at a private hospital in Punjab. A patient, Jiwan Lal, who was admitted to the hospital in a serious condition, was allegedly given an empty oxygen cylinder after his condition deteriorated. When the family detected the empty cylinder, they alerted hospital staff, but there was a significant delay in replacing it. The patient died shortly thereafter. A criminal case was registered against Dr. Jacob Mathew and the hospital's managing director under Section 304A of the Indian Penal Code (IPC), which pertains to causing death by a rash or negligent act. The case reached the Supreme Court on the question of whether a criminal prosecution could be sustained in such circumstances.

Issues Raised

Whether the facts of the case disclosed sufficient grounds to prosecute a doctor under Section 304A IPC for criminal negligence. What is the distinction between civil negligence (giving rise to compensation) and criminal negligence sufficient to attract Section

304A. What procedural safeguards should be observed before arresting or prosecuting medical professionals.

Arguments - Complainant / Appellant

The State argued that the administration of oxygen from an empty cylinder to a critical patient, and the delay in replacing it, amounted to rash and negligent conduct directly resulting in the patient's death, thereby attracting criminal liability under Section 304A IPC.

Arguments - Respondent

The appellant and medical community argued that doctors operate in difficult conditions, that errors in judgment are inevitable, and that criminalising medical mistakes would deter doctors from taking up difficult cases, ultimately harming patients. They contended that not every adverse medical outcome amounts to criminal recklessness.

Judgment & Ruling

The Supreme Court, in a landmark three-judge bench decision, quashed the criminal proceedings against Dr. Jacob Mathew under Section 304A IPC. The Court laid down authoritative guidelines distinguishing between civil negligence and criminal negligence in medical cases. It held that for criminal liability to attach, the negligence must be 'gross' - such as a departure from a standard of care so reckless that it shows wanton disregard for human life. The Court also issued procedural guidelines to prevent frivolous criminal prosecutions of doctors, mandating that a prior opinion of a competent medical expert be obtained before arrest or prosecution.

Key Holdings:

- Criminal negligence requires gross negligence, not mere error of judgment.

- The Bolam test applies in assessing medical negligence.
- An unsuccessful treatment does not by itself prove negligence.
- Doctors are judged by the standard of a reasonably competent professional.
- Independent medical opinion is required before prosecuting a doctor.
- Doctors should not be arrested routinely in negligence cases.
- Civil and criminal negligence have different standards of liability.
- The Court laid down safeguards to prevent frivolous criminal prosecution of doctors.

KEY LEGAL PRINCIPLES / RATIO DECIDENDI

- A doctor cannot be held criminally liable under Section 304A IPC unless the negligence is gross - that is, falling so far below the standard of reasonable care as to constitute culpable rashness or recklessness.
- Simple lack of care, an error of judgment, or choosing one reasonable treatment over another does not amount to criminal negligence.
- The Bolam test applies to the determination of whether a medical practitioner has departed from acceptable medical practice.
- Before arresting a doctor accused of criminal negligence, a competent medical authority's opinion should be obtained.
- No doctor should be arrested in a routine case of alleged medical negligence without prima facie evidence of gross negligence.

➲ A doctor acting in good faith and with due care, even if the outcome is fatal, shall not be subjected to criminal prosecution.

Compensation / Outcome

Criminal proceedings against Dr. Jacob Mathew were quashed. The Supreme Court issued a series of guidelines that now govern the prosecution of medical professionals under Section 304A IPC, which have since been extended also to civil proceedings.

Significance & Impact

Jacob Mathew v. State of Punjab is the most frequently cited and authoritative judgment on medical negligence in Indian jurisprudence. It fundamentally shaped the legal landscape by drawing a clear line between civil and criminal negligence in the medical context, protecting bona fide medical practitioners from harassment, while preserving accountability for gross professional misconduct. Every subsequent medico-legal case in India - civil, criminal, or before consumer fora - references this judgment.

MEDLEX360 PRACTICE PEARLS	
What went wrong?	A patient died, leading to criminal negligence proceedings against doctors.
Risk Management Takeaways	• Follow accepted standards of care. • Avoid shortcuts in critical care • Maintain complete treatment records • Seek specialist opinion when needed
Documentation Checklist	• Clinical notes • Treatment rationale • Specialist consultations

A bad outcome is not negligence, but poor documentation can make it appear so.

6. Samira Kohli

Full Case Name	Samira Kohli v. Dr. Prabha Manchanda & Anr.
Citation / Case Number	Civil Appeal No. 1949 of 2004 | (2008) 2 SCC 1 | AIR 2008 SC 1385 | 1(2008) CPJ 56 (SC)
Court / Forum	Supreme Court of India
Date of Judgment	16 January 2008
State / Jurisdiction	Delhi
Type of Case	Civil / Consumer Protection (Informed Consent)

Background & Facts

The appellant, Ms. Samira Kohli, was an unmarried woman aged 44 years. She consulted the respondent, Dr. Prabha Manchanda, a gynaecologist based in Delhi, on 9 May 1995, complaining of prolonged menstrual bleeding. After an ultrasound examination, Dr. Manchanda advised diagnostic laparoscopy under general anaesthesia. On 10 May 1995, the appellant was admitted and signed consent forms for 'diagnostic and operative laparoscopy; laparotomy may be needed.' While the appellant was under general anaesthesia, the respondent obtained the signature of the appellant's mother and performed an abdominal hysterectomy with bilateral salpingo-oophorectomy (AH-BSO), removing the uterus, both ovaries, and fallopian tubes. The appellant filed a complaint before the NCDRC on 19 January 1996, seeking ₹ 25 lakh compensation. The NCDRC dismissed the complaint in 2003, which was then appealed to the Supreme Court.

Issues Raised

Whether valid and specific informed consent of the patient was obtained before performing the extensive surgery to remove the reproductive organs. Whether consent for a diagnostic procedure can be construed as consent for additional radical therapeutic surgery. Whether consent obtained from a competent adult patient's relative is valid for elective surgery.

Arguments - Complainant / Appellant

The appellant argued that she had consented only to diagnostic laparoscopy and had not been specifically informed of, nor consented to, the possibility of a full hysterectomy and removal of ovaries. She contended that obtaining her mother's consent while she was unconscious was legally invalid. The surgery caused premature menopause, permanent loss of reproductive capacity, diminished matrimonial prospects, and severe emotional and physical trauma.

Arguments - Respondent

Dr. Manchanda argued that during diagnostic laparoscopy, extensive endometriosis was discovered and that the hysterectomy was medically necessary. She contended that the patient had implicitly consented to necessary operative procedures and that obtaining the mother's signature served as documentation of communication.

Judgment & Ruling

The Supreme Court allowed the appeal and held that the respondent doctor was guilty of deficiency in service and violation of the patient's right to informed consent. The Court held that consent for diagnostic surgery cannot be stretched to cover additional radical therapeutic procedures unless there is a life-threatening emergency. A competent adult patient's specific consent is mandatory for any procedure involving permanent or significant alteration of the body. Obtaining the consent of a relative while the patient is under general anaesthesia does not substitute for the patient's own prior informed consent for elective procedures.

Key Holdings:

- Valid informed consent is mandatory before any surgical procedure.
- Consent for diagnosis is not consent for surgery.
- A competent adult's consent cannot be replaced by a relative's consent, except in emergencies.
- Additional surgery without consent is permissible only in life-threatening emergencies.
- Doctors must disclose material information about the procedure, risks, benefits, and alternatives.
- India follows the doctrine of "real consent," not the stricter American standard of informed consent.
- Unauthorized surgery amounts to deficiency in service and attracts liability.
- The patient was awarded compensation for the unauthorized hysterectomy and related surgery.

KEY LEGAL PRINCIPLES / RATIO DECIDENDI

➲ A patient's right to give informed consent to any medical procedure is a fundamental aspect of personal autonomy and bodily integrity.

➲ Informed consent requires that the patient be made aware of the nature of the proposed procedure, its risks, the alternatives available, and the consequences of not proceeding.

➲ Consent obtained for one procedure (diagnostic) does not extend to additional elective procedures (therapeutic) without specific prior authorisation from the conscious patient.

- For elective procedures, consent of a relative does not substitute for the patient's own consent when the patient is a competent adult.
- The exception to the requirement of prior consent exists only in genuine life-threatening emergencies where it is impossible to obtain prior consent.

Compensation / Outcome

The Supreme Court awarded a compensation of ₹ 25,000 to the appellant - a modest amount given the period and the compensation claimed - and held the respondent liable for medical negligence and deficiency in service arising from failure to obtain proper informed consent.

Significance & Impact

This is India's most authoritative judgment on informed consent in medical practice. It established that the right to informed consent is a patient's fundamental right grounded in personal autonomy and bodily integrity. The judgment profoundly influenced medical practice guidelines in India, leading to more robust consent protocols in hospitals. It is universally cited in all subsequent Indian cases involving issues of patient consent.

MEDLEX360 PRACTICE PEARLS	
What went wrong?	A radical surgery was performed without obtaining the patient's specific informed consent.
Risk Management Takeaways	• Risk Management Takeaways • Obtain procedure-specific consent. • Discuss risks, benefits, and alternatives.

	• Do not rely on relative consent for elective surgery. • Respect patient autonomy. • Re-consent whenever circumstances permit.
Documentation Checklist	• Detailed consent form • Consent discussion notes • Risks explained • Alternatives discussed • Patient questions documented • Witness signature • Procedure-specific consent

Consent is a conversation, not a signature.

7. Malay Kumar Ganguly

Full Case Name	Malay Kumar Ganguly v. Dr. Sukumar Mukherjee & Ors.
Citation / Case Number	Criminal Appeal Nos. 1191-1194 of 2005; Civil Appeal No. 1727 of 2007 | (2009) 9 SCC 221 | [2009] INSC 1410
Court / Forum	Supreme Court of India
Date of Judgment	07 August 2009
State / Jurisdiction	West Bengal
Type of Case	Criminal and Civil

Background & Facts

This case arose from the same tragic events involving the death of Dr. Anuradha Saha, wife of Dr. Kunal Saha. The criminal appeals were filed by the State of West Bengal and by Malay Kumar Ganguly (brother-in-law) against the doctors (Dr. Sukumar Mukherjee, Dr. Baidyanath Haldar, Dr. Balram Prasad) and AMRI Hospital, Kolkata, who were accused of causing her death through negligent treatment of Toxic Epidermal Necrolysis (TEN) - a life-threatening skin disorder. The primary issue was the administration of excessive doses of Depomedrol (a steroid) to a TEN patient, which expert evidence later established was contra-indicated and was a departure from standard medical practice.

Issues Raised

Whether the conduct of thc trcating doctors in administering excessive steroids to a TEN patient constituted criminal negligence under Section 304A IPC. Whether the criminal and civil proceedings could be tried simultaneously. The standard of proof required to establish criminal liability in medical negligence cases.

Arguments - Complainant / Appellant

The appellants argued that the doctors had administered Depomedrol injections in a quantity and frequency that was widely known to be dangerous for TEN patients, and that this constituted rash and negligent conduct within the meaning of Section 304A IPC. Expert evidence was adduced to demonstrate that the treatment adopted was contrary to accepted medical protocols for TEN.

Arguments - Respondent

The respondent doctors contended that they had acted in good faith according to their clinical judgment, that TEN is itself a life-threatening disease, and that the treatment given was not demonstrably outside accepted practice at the time.

Judgment & Ruling

The Supreme Court found the treatment to constitute gross medical negligence and examined the standards governing criminal liability in medical negligence cases. The Court reiterated the test from Jacob Mathew: criminal liability attaches when negligence is so gross as to show disregard for patient safety. The Court also addressed the standards for expert evidence in medical cases and confirmed that expert testimony must emanate from individuals with relevant specialisation and must be objective.

Key Holdings:

- Medical negligence was established due to improper diagnosis and treatment.
- Doctors must follow accepted medical protocols and exercise reasonable care.
- Deviation from standard treatment may constitute negligence if it causes harm.

- Expert medical evidence is crucial in determining negligence.
- Consumer forums may award compensation for medical negligence.
- Civil and criminal liability have different standards of proof.
- Hospitals may be vicariously liable for the negligence of their doctors.
- Compensation should fairly reflect the injury suffered by the patient or family.

KEY LEGAL PRINCIPLES / RATIO DECIDENDI

- Criminal liability under Section 304A IPC requires proof of gross negligence - conduct so reckless that it shows wanton disregard for patient safety.
- Expert evidence in medical negligence cases must be rendered by a specialist in the relevant field; general medical qualifications do not suffice.
- The court may draw adverse inferences where medical records are tampered with or withheld.
- Concurrent civil and criminal proceedings arising from the same medical negligence are permissible.
- A hospital may be held vicariously liable for the acts of its consulting doctors under the Consumer Protection Act.

Compensation / Outcome

The Supreme Court found the doctors and AMRI Hospital guilty of negligence in the criminal proceedings and awarded compensation in the civil proceedings. The case was later reconsidered in Balram Prasad v. Kunal Saha (2013), which significantly enhanced the compensation to Dr. Kunal Saha to ₹ 5.96 crore (total with interest amounting to approximately ₹ 11.41 crore).

Significance & Impact

This judgment is pivotal for several reasons: it is one of the rare cases in India where a doctor was found criminally liable for medical negligence; it addresses the concurrent trial of criminal and civil proceedings; and it established rigorous standards for the appreciation of expert evidence in medico-legal proceedings. It complemented Jacob Mathew by detailing when the threshold for criminal liability is crossed.

MEDLEX360 PRACTICE PEARLS	
What went wrong?	Treatment deviated from accepted protocols and expert evidence established gross negligence.
Risk Management Takeaways	• Follow evidence-based protocols. • Document reasons for any deviation. • Seek multidisciplinary opinions in complex cases • Preserve records carefully • Never alter medical records.
Documentation Checklist	• Treatment protocol • Specialist opinions • Drug administration records

When you depart from guidelines, document why

8. Nizam's Institute

Full Case Name	Nizam's Institute of Medical Sciences v. Prasanth S. Dhananka & Ors.
Citation / Case Number	Civil Appeal No. 4119 of 1999 and Civil Appeal No. 3126 of 2000 | (2009) 6 SCC 1 | 2010 ACJ 38
Court / Forum	Supreme Court of India (Three-Judge Bench)
Date of Judgment	14 May 2009
State / Jurisdiction	Telangana (Andhra Pradesh)
Type of Case	Civil / Consumer Protection

Background & Facts

Prasanth S. Dhananka, the complainant, was a young engineer with a bright career ahead. He was admitted to NIMS (Nizam's Institute of Medical Sciences), Hyderabad, for removal of a tumour from his chest (right side). During the surgical procedure, the surgeons caused damage to the spinal cord, resulting in permanent paraplegia - complete and irreversible loss of use of both lower limbs. He filed a complaint before the NCDRC, which found negligence and awarded compensation. Both parties appealed to the Supreme Court - NIMS challenging the finding of negligence, and the complainant seeking enhanced compensation.

Issues Raised

Whether the damage to the spinal cord during surgery constituted medical negligence. What principles govern the assessment and quantification of compensation in cases of permanent disability caused by medical negligence.

Arguments - Complainant / Appellant

The complainant argued that the damage to the spinal cord was preventable with due care and that the surgical team failed to exercise adequate caution during the procedure. He contended that the compensation awarded by the NCDRC was grossly inadequate given the devastating and permanent nature of his disability and the loss of his career prospects.

Arguments - Respondent

NIMS contended that the surgery was performed in accordance with accepted norms and that the spinal cord injury was an unfortunate risk inherent to the procedure, not attributable to negligence. It was argued that the compensation awarded was excessive.

Judgment & Ruling

The Supreme Court confirmed the finding of negligence against NIMS, holding that where the complainant establishes a strong prima facie case and the relevant medical facts lie especially within the knowledge of the hospital, the evidentiary burden may shift to the hospital to explain the treatment provided. The Court formulated important principles for computing compensation in disability cases, directing that compensation must be holistic - accounting for loss of earning capacity (current and future), the cost of continued medical care, the impact on personal and family life, and the patient's quality of life. The Court significantly enhanced the compensation awarded.

Key Holdings:

- Medical negligence was established due to lapses in pre-operative and operative care.

- Hospitals are vicariously liable for the negligence of their doctors.
- Consent for one procedure is not implied consent for a more extensive surgery.
- Withholding medical records permits an adverse inference against the hospital.
- Once a prima facie case is shown, the burden shifts to the hospital to disprove negligence.
- Compensation should reflect lifelong disability and future care needs.
- The multiplier method is not mandatory in medical negligence compensation cases.
- The Supreme Court enhanced compensation to ₹1 crore considering the catastrophic injury suffered.

KEY LEGAL PRINCIPLES / RATIO DECIDENDI

➲ In medical negligence cases, once the complainant establishes a prima facie case of negligence, the burden of proof shifts to the hospital/doctor to disprove it.

➲ Compensation must be 'just and reasonable' and must account for past and future medical expenses, loss of earning capacity, pain and suffering, and loss of amenities of life.

➲ An award of compensation that is either grossly inflated or unreasonably nominal is itself susceptible to challenge; courts must strive for a just mean.

➲ A young person's loss of earning capacity due to permanent disability must be computed on the basis of future prospects, not just current income.

➲ Hospitals bear vicarious liability for negligent acts of their employed or engaged medical staff.

Compensation / Outcome

The Supreme Court confirmed the finding of negligence against NIMS and substantially enhanced the compensation to ₹ 1 crore (a landmark quantum at the time), acknowledging the devastating and permanent nature of the injury and its impact on the complainant's life and career.

Significance & Impact

This judgment is a landmark in the jurisprudence of compensation for permanent disability arising from medical negligence in India. It established the principle that compensation must be assessed holistically and must be adequate to address the lifelong consequences of disability. The shift-of-burden principle articulated in this case is now a standard feature of Indian medical negligence jurisprudence.

MEDLEX360 PRACTICE PEARLS	
What went wrong?	A preventable surgical injury resulted in permanent disability.
Risk Management Takeaways	• Discuss major operative risks honestly. • Use surgical safety protocols rigorously. • Escalate concerns immediately. • Maintain long-term follow-up documentation. • Understand the lifelong consequences of disability claims.
Documentation Checklist	• Risk counselling • Operative notes • Post-operative monitoring records

The larger the risk, the stronger the documentation

9. Martin F. D'Souza

Full Case Name	Martin F. D'Souza v. Mohd. Ishfaq
Citation / Case Number	(2009) 3 SCC 1 | JT 2009 (2) SC 486
Court / Forum	Supreme Court of India
Date of Judgment	17 February 2009
State / Jurisdiction	Delhi
Type of Case	Civil / Consumer Protection

Background & Facts

The complainant, Mohd. Ishfaq, filed a complaint against Dr. Martin F. D'Souza, a nephrologist, alleging that his treatment resulted in injury. The case came up before a two-judge bench of the Supreme Court. The Court took the opportunity to address systemic concerns about the rapid increase of medical negligence complaints before consumer fora and the impact of such litigation on the medical profession.

Issues Raised

Whether complaints filed before consumer fora under the Consumer Protection Act require expert evidence before being admitted. Whether all complaints of medical negligence must be referred to an expert medical committee prior to being entertained by consumer fora.

Arguments - Complainant / Appellant

The complainant alleged that the treatment administered by the nephrologist was negligent and caused him harm, for which compensation was sought under the Consumer Protection Act.

Arguments - Respondent

The doctor denied negligence and argued that the treatment was in accordance with accepted medical standards. There was also a broader argument that the increasing incidence of frivolous medical negligence complaints was having a chilling effect on medical practice in India.

Judgment & Ruling

The Supreme Court in this judgment - authored by a two-judge bench - went beyond the specific facts and issued a general direction that consumer fora, prior to entertaining any complaint of medical negligence, should first obtain an opinion from a medical expert committee. This direction was subsequently declared per incuriam (wrongly decided) by a three-judge bench of the Supreme Court in V. Kishan Rao v. Nikhil Super Speciality Hospital (2010), which held that the direction in D'Souza was contrary to the earlier three-judge bench decision in Jacob Mathew. The direction requiring mandatory expert committee opinion before entertaining medical negligence complaints is no longer good law after V. Kishan Rao v. Nikhil Super Speciality Hospital (2010).

Key Holdings:

- Medical negligence must be proved with credible evidence, not presumed from an adverse outcome.
- The Bolam test governs the standard of medical negligence.
- Consumer forums should obtain an independent expert opinion before issuing notice in medical negligence cases.
- Doctors are not liable if they follow an accepted medical practice.
- A mere error of judgment is not negligence.
- Medical professionals deserve protection from frivolous and vexatious complaints.

- Courts should avoid hindsight while evaluating a doctor's conduct.
- The Supreme Court set aside the finding of negligence against the doctor on the facts of the case.

KEY LEGAL PRINCIPLES / RATIO DECIDENDI

➲ Consumer fora have jurisdiction to hear complaints of medical negligence under the Consumer Protection Act.

➲ The principle that expert evidence is necessary in complicated medical cases was addressed, though the mandatory referral direction was later overruled.

➲ Frivolous and vexatious complaints against medical professionals cause harm to the profession and should be carefully screened.

➲ Note: The specific direction to refer all complaints to an expert committee was declared per incuriam in V. Kishan Rao (2010).

Compensation / Outcome

In the specific case, the complaint was disposed of on merits. However, the broader directions issued in this judgment regarding mandatory expert committee referral were subsequently overturned by a larger bench.

Significance & Impact

Martin D'Souza v. Mohd. Ishfaq is significant for two reasons: first, for its articulation of the concerns about the medico-legal relationship and the burden of litigation on the medical profession; and second, for its role in the subsequent jurisprudential development when its key directions were declared per incuriam by a three-judge bench in V. Kishan Rao (2010), thereby clarifying the precedential hierarchy in medical negligence law.

MEDLEX360 PRACTICE PEARLS	
What went wrong?	The case highlighted concerns about frivolous negligence claims.
Risk Management Takeaways	• Maintain professional standards at all times. • Document clinical reasoning. • Avoid defensive medicine. • Communicate expectations clearly. • Preserve records for future review.
Documentation Checklist	• Diagnostic reasoning • Treatment justification • Follow-up records

Clinical judgment is easier to defend when it is documented.

10. Nikhil Super Speciality Hospital

Full Case Name	V. Kishan Rao v. Nikhil Super Speciality Hospital & Anr.
Citation / Case Number	Civil Appeal No. 2641 of 2010 (arising from SLP(C) No. 15084 of 2009) | (2010) 5 SCC 513
Court / Forum	Supreme Court of India
Date of Judgment	08 March 2010
State / Jurisdiction	Andhra Pradesh (Hyderabad)
Type of Case	Civil / Consumer Protection

Background & Facts

The appellant's wife was admitted to Nikhil Super Speciality Hospital, Hyderabad, on 20 July 2002, suffering from fever that was intermittent in nature with chills. The patient was treated for malaria by the hospital, and her condition deteriorated. She was subsequently transferred to another hospital where she was diagnosed with typhoid, not malaria. She died thereafter. The appellant filed a complaint before the District Consumer Forum, which found negligence and awarded compensation. However, both the State Consumer Commission and the NCDRC overturned the finding, holding that no expert evidence had been produced by the complainant to establish negligence.

Issues Raised

Whether the requirement of expert evidence is mandatory in every case of alleged medical negligence before consumer fora. Whether the direction in Martin F. D'Souza (2009) requiring mandatory expert committee referral was good law.

Arguments - Complainant / Appellant

The appellant argued that misdiagnosing typhoid as malaria when the disease could have been diagnosed by a simple Widal test or blood culture was itself evidence of negligence requiring no further expert testimony, and that the consumer fora were wrong to demand expert evidence for such straightforward cases.

Arguments - Respondent

The hospital contended that diagnosing fever with intermittent features requires clinical judgment, that differential diagnoses exist, and that the complainant had not led expert evidence to prove that the treatment fell below the standard of care.

Judgment & Ruling

The Supreme Court, in a detailed judgment, declared the directions in Martin F. D'Souza v. Mohd. Ishfaq (2009) as per incuriam - i.e., wrongly decided - on the ground that the two-judge bench in D'Souza had not followed the binding three-judge bench authority in Jacob Mathew. The Court held that consumer fora are not required to mandatorily refer every medical negligence complaint to an expert committee before entertaining it. The Court restored the District Forum's finding of negligence, holding that in this case, the misdiagnosis of typhoid as malaria was not consistent with basic expected standards.

Key Holdings:

- Expert evidence is not mandatory in every medical negligence case before consumer forums.
- Consumer forums may decide cases without expert opinion where negligence is apparent from the facts.
- The requirement of expert evidence depends on case facts and cannot be applied mechanically.

- The Bolam test remains the standard for assessing medical negligence.
- Consumer forums have discretion to call for expert evidence when necessary.
- The Court disagreed with the mandatory expert-opinion requirement laid down in *Martin F. D'Souza v. Mohd. Ishfaq*.
- Medical negligence was found on the facts of the case, and compensation awarded by the District Forum was restored.
- The judgment strengthened access to consumer remedies by preventing unnecessary barriers in medical negligence claims.

KEY LEGAL PRINCIPLES / RATIO DECIDENDI

- Consumer fora are competent to determine medical negligence complaints without mandatory prior reference to an expert committee.
- In straightforward cases of alleged negligence, consumer fora may use common sense and general reasoning without necessarily requiring expert medical testimony.
- The judgment in Martin F. D'Souza (2009) directing mandatory referral of all medical complaints to expert committees was declared per incuriam.
- A two-judge bench cannot overrule or deviate from the decision of a three-judge bench.
- Failure to diagnose a condition readily detectable by standard investigations may itself constitute evidence of negligence.

Compensation / Outcome

The Supreme Court set aside the orders of the State Commission and NCDRC, restored the District Consumer Forum's finding of negligence, and directed the hospital to pay the compensation awarded by the District Forum. The judgment also effectively overruled the mandatory expert referral directions from Martin D'Souza.

Significance & Impact

This judgment is critical in the evolution of Indian medical negligence law. By declaring D'Souza per incuriam and reinstating access to consumer fora without mandatory expert committee barriers, the Court preserved the accessibility of the consumer protection framework for medical negligence victims. It remains the authoritative position on the question of expert evidence in consumer proceedings for medical negligence.

MEDLEX360 PRACTICE PEARLS	
What went wrong?	Failure to diagnose a readily identifiable condition resulted in liability.
Risk Management Takeaways	• Rule out common diagnoses before assuming rare ones. • Order indicated investigations promptly. • Reassess when patients fail to improve. • Escalate unresolved cases. • Follow diagnostic protocols.
Documentation Checklist	• Differential diagnosis • Investigation reports • Follow-up assessment notes

Missed diagnoses often begin with missed reassessments

11. Kusum Sharma

Full Case Name	Kusum Sharma & Others v. Batra Hospital & Medical Research Centre & Others
Citation / Case Number	Civil Appeal No. 1385 of 2001 | (2010) 3 SCC 480 | AIR 2010 SC 1050
Court / Forum	Supreme Court of India
Date of Judgment	10 February 2010
State / Jurisdiction	Delhi
Type of Case	Civil / Consumer Protection

Background & Facts

Shri R.K. Sharma, Senior Operations Manager at Indian Oil Corporation, was diagnosed in June 1989 with a left adrenal tumour suspected to be malignant. He was admitted to Batra Hospital, New Delhi, where the surgery was performed. Post-operatively, he developed complications and ultimately died. His widow, Kusum Sharma, and their children filed a complaint under Section 21 of the Consumer Protection Act, 1986, before the NCDRC claiming compensation of ₹ 45 lakhs, alleging deficiency in services and medical negligence during treatment. The NCDRC dismissed the complaint. The case reached the Supreme Court.

Issues Raised

Whether the treatment given by Batra Hospital and its doctors to the deceased fell below the standard of carc cxpected of a competent medical professional. What are the comprehensive principles governing the determination of medical negligence in India?

Arguments - Complainant / Appellant

The appellants argued that the post-operative management of the patient was negligent, that there was undue delay in diagnosing and treating complications, and that these failures directly contributed to the patient's death.

Arguments - Respondent

The hospital and doctors contended that the surgery was performed appropriately, that post-operative complications arose from the underlying malignancy, and that the treatment at all stages was consistent with accepted medical practice.

Judgment & Ruling

The Supreme Court dismissed the appeal, finding no negligence on the part of the hospital or doctors. However, the judgment is celebrated not for its specific outcome but for its comprehensive and authoritative consolidation of the principles governing medical negligence in India. Justice Dalveer Bhandari enunciated eleven cardinal principles that must be kept in mind while deciding medical negligence cases.

Key Holdings:

- Negligence requires breach of duty: Mere failure or adverse outcome does not prove medical negligence.
- Doctors need reasonable skill and care, not the highest possible standard.
- Error of judgment is not negligence if the doctor follows an accepted medical practice.
- Medical decisions are judged by standards existing at the time of treatment, not with hindsight.
- The Bolam test applies for assessing professional medical negligence.

- Courts must protect doctors from frivolous claims while ensuring genuine negligence is addressed.
- Doctors are not negligent for choosing one accepted treatment option over another.
- No negligence was proved in the case; the complaint against the hospital and doctors was dismissed.

KEY LEGAL PRINCIPLES / RATIO DECIDENDI

- A medical professional is not liable to be found negligent simply because something went wrong or did not succeed.
- Negligence cannot be attributed merely because in hindsight a better treatment was available.
- The standard of care is that of the ordinary competent doctor exercising the ordinary degree of professional skill.
- The test is whether the professional acted in accordance with a practice accepted by a responsible body of medical opinion (Bolam test).
- A doctor may be held liable for negligence in respect of diagnosis and treatment, notwithstanding adherence to a common practice, if the practice itself is found to be contrary to plain precaution or logic (Bolitho qualification).
- Courts and consumer fora must not substitute their own views for those of medical experts on purely technical or clinical questions.
- Compensation to victims of medical negligence should be 'just and reasonable' and not punitive.
- The benefit of doubt, in absence of clear proof, must be given to the doctor in cases involving choice of treatment.
- Medical professionals deserve protection from frivolous and vexatious litigation.
- Both the doctor's professional duty and the patient's right to correct treatment are fundamental interests that courts must balance.

➲ Hospitals are vicariously liable for the acts of their employed physicians.

Compensation / Outcome

The Supreme Court dismissed the appeal of the complainants. The hospital and doctors were absolved of liability in this specific case.

Significance & Impact

Kusum Sharma v. Batra Hospital is perhaps the most comprehensive treatise on the law of medical negligence in India by the Supreme Court. Its eleven-principle framework is routinely quoted by every court, consumer forum, and tribunal across the country as the definitive statement of the law. It synthesised decades of jurisprudence into a coherent, accessible framework and is considered a must-cite authority in every medical negligence matter.

MEDLEX360 PRACTICE PEARLS	
What went wrong?	The allegation failed because negligence was not proved.
Risk Management Takeaways	• Practice according to accepted standards. • Avoid hindsight-based decision-making. • Keep evidence of clinical judgment. • Record patient discussions. • Stay updated with accepted medical practice.
Documentation Checklist	• Clinical reasoning • Expert consultations • Progress notes

Courts judge reasonableness, not perfection

12. Balram Prasad

Full Case Name	Dr. Balram Prasad v. Dr. Kunal Saha & Ors. (and connected matters)
Citation / Case Number	Civil Appeal No. 2867 of 2012, Civil Appeal No. 692 of 2012, Civil Appeal No. 2866 of 2012 | (2014) 1 SCC 384 | 2013 (13) SCALE 1
Court / Forum	Supreme Court of India
Date of Judgment	24 October 2013
State / Jurisdiction	West Bengal
Type of Case	Civil / Consumer Protection

Background & Facts

This is the final chapter in the long legal saga initiated by Dr. Kunal Saha following the death of his wife, Dr. Anuradha Saha, in May 1998. Anuradha had developed Toxic Epidermal Necrolysis (TEN), a fatal skin disorder. She was treated by Dr. Sukumar Mukherjee and colleagues at AMRI Hospital, Kolkata. Expert opinion established that Depomedrol (a steroid) was contraindicated for TEN patients, yet it was administered repeatedly. Anuradha died on 28 May 1998 at Breach Candy Hospital, Mumbai, where she had been airlifted. After 15 years of litigation, the case culminated in a Supreme Court judgment on compensation.

Issues Raised

What quantum of compensation is just and reasonable for the wrongful death of a young professional woman due to medical negligence? Whether contributory negligence of the husband (Dr. Kunal Saha) was established. How should compensation be apportioned among multiple negligent parties (hospital and individual doctors)?

Arguments - Complainant / Appellant

Dr. Kunal Saha sought an enhancement of the NCDRC's compensation of ₹ 1.73 crore to reflect the true loss suffered, including the loss of a partner who was herself a qualified professional with substantial earning potential, and damages for pain, suffering, and the prolonged agony of the litigation.

Arguments - Respondent

The doctors and hospital sought reduction of the compensation, contending that the NCDRC had exaggerated the award, and some argued that Dr. Saha's own actions (including delay in evacuation) contributed to the death.

Judgment & Ruling

The Supreme Court enhanced the compensation from ₹ 1.73 crore (awarded by the NCDRC in 2011) to ₹ 5.96 crore, with interest at 6% per annum from 1999, making the total payable approximately ₹ 11.41 crore. The Court exonerated Dr. Kunal Saha from any contributory negligence. AMRI Hospital was held vicariously liable for the negligence of its consulting doctors. The Court laid down important principles on the computation of compensation in wrongful death cases.

Key Holdings:

- Medical negligence was established against the doctors and hospital for improper treatment of the patient.
- Hospitals and doctors can be held jointly liable for negligence causing patient harm.
- Patients have a right to dignified treatment as part of their human and fundamental rights.
- Compensation must be just and reasonable, considering loss of income, suffering, and future consequences.

- Consumer forums can award substantial compensation in cases of serious medical negligence.
- Interest may be awarded on compensation from the date of filing the complaint until payment.
- Hospitals and medical establishments must maintain accountability and may require stricter regulation.
- Medical negligence cases require careful assessment of professional duty, breach, and resulting harm.

KEY LEGAL PRINCIPLES / RATIO DECIDENDI

➲ A hospital is vicariously liable for the negligent acts of consulting doctors retained by it, even if they are not permanent employees.

➲ Contributory negligence of the patient or family must be specifically proved by the defendant and cannot be presumed.

➲ Compensation for wrongful death must account for the income of the deceased (actual and prospective), loss of consortium, and the nature of the relationship.

➲ Where multiple defendants are found negligent, the court has jurisdiction to apportion liability.

➲ Interest on compensation runs from the date of the cause of action (not just from the date of the order) to ensure full restitution.

Compensation / Outcome

₹ 5.96 crore principal compensation awarded to Dr. Kunal Saha, with interest at 6% per annum from 1999, total payout approximately ₹ 11.41 crore - the highest compensation awarded in an Indian medical negligence case at that time.

Significance & Impact

Balram Prasad v. Kunal Saha set a historic benchmark for compensation in medical negligence cases in India and remains the highest compensation ever awarded. It validated the principle that financial redress must genuinely reflect the loss suffered and must not be nominal. The case also powerfully demonstrated the importance of patient advocacy and the right to pursue justice, even across fifteen years of litigation.

MEDLEX360 PRACTICE PEARLS	
What went wrong?	Negligent treatment led to one of India's highest compensation awards.
Risk Management Takeaways	• Never underestimate the financial impact of negligence. • Follow evidence-based treatment pathways. • Maintain transparent communication with families. • Preserve all records indefinitely in serious cases. • Review high-risk cases internally.
Documentation Checklist	• Treatment chronology • Family communication notes • Consent and referral records

The cost of negligence is often measured decades later.

13. Maharaja Agrasen Hospital

Full Case Name	Maharaja Agrasen Hospital & Ors. v. Master Rishabh Sharma & Ors. | Pooja Sharma & Ors. v. Maharaja Agrasen Hospital & Ors.
Citation / Case Number	Civil Appeal No. 6619 of 2016 and Civil Appeal No. 9461 of 2019 | Decided on 16 December 2019
Court / Forum	Supreme Court of India
Date of Judgment	16 December 2019
State / Jurisdiction	Delhi
Type of Case	Civil / Consumer Protection

Background & Facts

Master Rishabh Sharma was a premature infant born at Maharaja Agrasen Hospital, New Delhi. As per established neonatal care protocols, premature babies are at high risk of Retinopathy of Prematurity (ROP), a potentially blinding eye condition, and must undergo mandatory ROP screening within specific timeframes after birth. The hospital's paediatricians failed to inform the parents of this mandatory screening requirement and failed to arrange the examination. As a direct consequence of this omission, the early-stage ROP went undiagnosed and untreated, progressing to total and irreversible blindness in the child. The family filed a consumer complaint before the NCDRC, which found the hospital and its doctors guilty of negligence.

Issues Raised

Whether the failure to conduct a mandatory ROP screen on a premature infant constitutes medical negligence. Whether a hospital is vicariously liable for medical negligence committed by its consulting or contracted specialists. What is the measure of compensation for permanent disability in a child?

Arguments - Complainant / Appellant

The parents argued that ROP screening is a universally mandated standard of neonatal care for premature infants, that the hospital failed to advise them of this requirement, and that this failure was the direct and proximate cause of their child's blindness. They contended that both the hospital and its engaged doctors were liable.

Arguments - Respondent

The hospital argued that it had engaged specialists in good faith, that the responsibility for advising ROP screening lay with the ophthalmologist, and sought to distance itself from vicarious liability. Individual doctors also denied being the responsible party.

Judgment & Ruling

The Supreme Court upheld the finding of negligence against the hospital and its doctors (paediatricians and ophthalmologist). The Court held that a hospital is vicariously liable for the medical negligence of doctors it employs or engages, whether on a permanent or consultancy basis. The Court affirmed that when a patient is admitted to a hospital, the patient and family place trust in the institution, not merely in an individual doctor. The failure to conduct a mandatory medical screening - one whose necessity is established by international clinical guidelines - constituted an open and shut case of medical negligence.

Key Holdings:

- Failure to conduct mandatory ROP screening was medical negligence resulting in permanent blindness of the child.

- Hospitals and doctors have a duty of care to follow established medical protocols for vulnerable patients.
- Negligence requires proof of duty, breach, and resulting injury.
- Hospitals are vicariously liable for negligence of doctors providing care under their authority.
- Medical negligence can be inferred where the hospital fails to produce evidence of following required procedures.
- Compensation must account for lifelong disability, future needs, and loss of quality of life.
- The hospital and doctors were held jointly and severally liable for payment of compensation.
- The Court emphasised patient welfare and accountability while assessing medical negligence claims.

KEY LEGAL PRINCIPLES / RATIO DECIDENDI

➲ A hospital is vicariously liable for the acts of omission and commission of doctors engaged or retained by it, regardless of their mode of engagement (full-time or contractual).

➲ Patients and families trust the hospital as an institution; the hospital cannot escape liability by attributing fault solely to individual doctors.

➲ The failure to comply with a mandatory, internationally recognised standard of neonatal care is prima facie evidence of negligence.

➲ Paediatricians attending on premature infants have a duty to advise parents of mandatory follow-up screenings such as ROP.

Compensation / Outcome

The Supreme Court upheld the finding of negligence and confirmed the compensation awarded by the NCDRC. The hospital and its doctors were held jointly and severally liable. Compensation was awarded including amounts for the child's lifetime care, education, and loss of quality of life.

Significance & Impact

This judgment reinforced and expanded the doctrine of vicarious liability of hospitals in India. It made clear that hospitals cannot use the contractual arrangement with doctors as a shield against liability. The case also highlighted the importance of adherence to evidence-based clinical guidelines in paediatric and neonatal care, and has been widely cited in subsequent cases involving hospital negligence.

MEDLEX360 PRACTICE PEARLS	
What went wrong?	The dispute focused on hospital liability and accountability for acts performed within the institutional healthcare system. The hospital's paediatricians failed to arrange the ROP examination. As a direct consequence of this omission, ROP went undiagnosed and untreated, progressing to total and irreversible blindness in the child.
Risk Management Takeaways	• Remember that hospitals are responsible for the systems they create • Ensure proper supervision of consultants and resident doctors • Maintain standardized treatment protocols • Conduct periodic quality audits • Develop a culture of patient safety

MEDLEX360 PRACTICE PEARLS	
Documentation Checklist	• Admission records • Clinical supervision notes • Hospital protocols followed

A strong hospital system is often the first line of medico-legal defence

14. Shiv Ram

Full Case Name	State of Punjab v. Shiv Ram & Ors.
Citation / Case Number	(2005) 7 SCC 1; AIR 2005 SC 3280; Civil Appeal No. 5128 of 2002
Court / Forum	Supreme Court of India
Date of Judgment	25 August 2005
State / Jurisdiction	Punjab
Type of Case	Civil Suit / Medical Negligence / Wrongful Birth / Failed Sterilisation

Background & Facts

Shiv Ram (Respondent No. 1) and his wife (Respondent No. 2) had been married for over 17 years and already had a son and two daughters - three children in total. In response to a government publicity campaign carried out by the Family Welfare Department of the State of Punjab, Respondent No. 2, with the full consent of her husband, underwent a tubectomy (female sterilisation) operation on 1 August 1984, performed by a lady surgeon employed at Civil Hospital, Bhatinda.

A formal sterilisation certificate bearing identification number 505 was issued by the operating surgeon after the procedure, confirming that the operation had been carried out.

Despite the sterilisation, Respondent No. 2 subsequently became pregnant and gave birth to a female child. The couple filed a civil suit against the State of Punjab (as the employer of the operating surgeon) and the lady surgeon herself, claiming damages of **₹3,00,000** on the ground that the birth of this unwanted child was the direct consequence of negligence in performing the tubectomy operation.

The trial court decreed the suit in the plaintiffs' favour solely on the ground that a pregnancy had occurred after the sterilisation - without making any finding of negligence in the actual performance of the surgery. This error was repeated by the first appellate court and the High Court, which both upheld the decree. The State of Punjab appealed to the Supreme Court.

Issues Raised

- Whether the birth of a child following a sterilisation operation is, by itself, sufficient to establish medical negligence on the part of the operating surgeon.
- Whether the doctrine of res ipsa loquitur (the thing speaks for itself) can be applied to a failed sterilisation to automatically impute negligence.
- What are the scientifically recognised causes of sterilisation failure, and which of those causes give rise to legal liability?
- When does a cause of action for compensation arise in failed sterilisation cases - upon the failure of the operation or upon proof of surgical negligence?
- Whether a child born after a failed sterilisation can be termed “unwanted” if the couple, upon learning of the pregnancy, opts to continue with it rather than seek medical termination.
- What policy considerations must courts bear in mind when adjudicating failed sterilisation cases arising from government family planning programmes?
- Whether the State should establish a welfare fund or insurance scheme for those who experience natural sterilisation failures.

Arguments - Appellant

- No court below made any finding that the lady surgeon was negligent, incompetent, or had deviated from the standard of care in performing the tubectomy. The decree rested entirely on the bare fact of post-sterilisation pregnancy.

- Medical science recognises that sterilisation operations are not 100% successful. Failure rates of 0.3% to 3% are documented in authoritative medical textbooks and are attributable to natural causes - not surgical error.
- The primary recognised natural cause is spontaneous recanalisation - the spontaneous reunion of the fallopian tubes after they have been surgically cut and sealed, a biological phenomenon that can occur even when the surgery was performed correctly.
- Other recognised causes include undetected pre-existing pregnancy at the time of surgery, and imperfect occlusion - but the latter, unlike the former, is attributable to the surgeon's technique and can constitute negligence.
- The plaintiffs did not allege, and no court below found, that the surgeon was incompetent or that the surgery was improperly performed.
- Upon learning of the pregnancy, the couple had the legal option to terminate the pregnancy under the Medical Termination of Pregnancy Act within 20 weeks. Their choice to continue the pregnancy and bear the child means the child is no longer "unwanted" in any legally cognisable sense.
- Awarding automatic damages for every failed sterilisation would have a chilling effect on government family planning programmes - doctors would be reluctant to perform sterilisations and the State would be reluctant to conduct family welfare camps, ultimately harming public health goals.

Arguments - Respondent

- The couple underwent the sterilisation specifically to prevent further pregnancies; a certificate was issued confirming the procedure.
- The subsequent pregnancy is direct evidence that the procedure either was not properly performed or failed due to negligence.

- The couple relied on the certificate and trusted the medical assurance. They should not bear the financial burden of an unwanted child caused by the failure of a procedure they underwent on the State's encouragement.
- Reliance was placed on *State of Haryana v. Smt. Santra* ((2000) 5 SCC 182), where the Supreme Court had upheld compensation for a failed sterilisation.
- The State, as the employer of the operating surgeon, is vicariously liable for the surgeon's negligence and the consequences thereof.

Judgment & Ruling

The Supreme Court held that the mere failure of a sterilisation (tubectomy) operation resulting in pregnancy does not by itself establish medical negligence. The Court observed that no sterilisation procedure guarantees 100% success, and pregnancy may occur despite the operation being performed with due skill and care. Therefore, liability arises only if the claimant proves that the doctor or hospital acted negligently in performing the procedure or providing post-operative care. As the respondents failed to prove negligence, the Supreme Court allowed the State's appeal, set aside the compensation awarded by the lower courts, and dismissed the suit, while directing that the ₹50,000 already paid to the respondents would not be recovered.

Key Holdings:

- **Failed Sterilisation ≠ Medical Negligence:**
  Post-sterilisation pregnancy does not, by itself, establish negligence. Child birth in spite of a sterilisation operation can occur due to negligence of the doctor in the performance of the operation, or due to certain natural causes such as spontaneous recanalisation. The doctor can be held liable only in cases where the failure of the operation is attributable to his negligence and not otherwise.

- **Res Ipsa Loquitur Does Not Apply to Sterilisation Failures:**
  The doctrine of res ipsa loquitur cannot be invoked merely because a pregnancy occurred after a sterilisation. The known, documented failure rate of sterilisation due to natural causes (0.3%-7% depending on technique) means that the occurrence of pregnancy is not, by itself, self-evident proof of negligence. The claim can only be sustained if negligence by the operating surgeon is affirmatively proved.

- **Recognised Causes of Sterilisation Failure - Three Categories:**
  The Court extensively reviewed authoritative medical texts and established three categories:
  i. **Non-negligent causes:** Spontaneous recanalisation and fistula formation - the tubes reunite naturally after surgery; this is a biological phenomenon beyond the surgeon's control
  ii. **Indefensible failures:** Undetected pregnancy at the time of surgery - this is an absolute obligation of the surgeon; pregnancy testing before sterilisation must be done.
  iii. **Technical failures potentially indicating negligence:** Imperfect occlusion of the tube - particularly in laparoscopic methods; if a ring or clip is not properly applied, and the surgeon fails to inform the patient and advise alternative contraception, this can constitute negligence. Discrepancy between operation notes and X-ray findings regarding the number of rings or clips used will lead to a logical inference of negligence.

- **Cause of Action Arises on Negligence, Not on Childbirth:**
  The cause of action for claiming compensation in cases of failed sterilisation operation arises on account of negligence

of the surgeon and not on account of child birth. Failure due to natural causes would not provide any ground for claim.

- **A Continued Pregnancy Is No Longer "Unwanted":** Having gathered the knowledge of conception in spite of having undergone sterilisation operation, if the couple opts for bearing the child, it ceases to be an unwanted child. Compensation for maintenance and upbringing of such a child cannot be claimed. Once the couple learns of the pregnancy and chooses not to terminate it within the legally permissible period (20 weeks under the MTP Act), the child's birth is a voluntary choice and cannot form the basis of a damages claim.

- **Santra Distinguished:** The *Smt. Santra* case (State of Haryana v. Smt. Santra) was distinguished. In that case, only one fallopian tube was operated upon, contrary to the patient's consent for bilateral sterilisation - an indefensible error. That judgment rested on its specific facts and did not lay down a universal rule of liability for all failed sterilisations.

- **Policy Observations - Welfare Fund Recommended:** The Court was concerned about the chilling effect of automatic liability on government family planning programmes. It observed that sterilisation failures due to natural causes should not expose surgeons and the State to legal liability. However, to balance this with the legitimate grievance of couples who experience natural failure, the Court recommended that State Governments should **devise a welfare fund or take up an insurance scheme** to provide ex gratia relief to such couples, without admitting any negligence.

Compensation / Outcome

The Supreme Court allowed the State of Punjab's appeal and set aside the judgments awarding damages to the respondents. It held that the mere failure of a sterilisation procedure, resulting in the birth of a child, does not automatically entitle a claimant to compensation. Liability arises only if medical negligence is proved in accordance with the Bolam test or if there was an express guarantee of complete sterility. Although the compensation award was quashed, the Court directed that the ₹50,000 already paid to the respondents would not be recovered by the State as a matter of equity.

Significance & Impact

State of Punjab v. Shiv Ram is a landmark decision that clarified the law on medical negligence in sterilisation-failure cases. The Court established that doctors are expected to exercise reasonable skill and care, not guarantee successful outcomes, thereby protecting medical practitioners from strict liability for inherent procedural failures. At the same time, it encouraged governments to consider welfare or insurance schemes to support families affected by genuine sterilisation failures, balancing patient welfare with realistic standards of medical liability.

KEY LEGAL PRINCIPLES / RATIO DECIDENDI

- This is a landmark judgment definitively settling the law on failed sterilisation in India.
- Prior to this judgment, courts at the trial and first appellate levels routinely awarded damages for failed sterilisation on the sole ground that a pregnancy occurred - applying res ipsa loquitur without any analysis of causation.

- The Supreme Court emphatically rejected this approach. The ratio is clear: (1) No method of sterilisation known to medical science is 100% successful. (2) Sterilisation can fail due to natural biological causes (spontaneous recanalisation) entirely beyond the surgeon's control. (3) The cause of action for compensation arises only when negligence by the operating surgeon is proved - not merely on account of pregnancy following the procedure. (4) Res ipsa loquitur does not apply to a phenomenon with a documented natural failure rate. (5) If a couple, upon learning of a post-sterilisation pregnancy, chooses to continue the pregnancy rather than seek MTP within 20 weeks, the child is no longer "unwanted" and compensation for its upbringing cannot be claimed.
- This case is paired invariably with *Jacob Mathew v. State of Punjab* (2005) 6 SCC 1 (decided in the same period by a coordinate bench) as defining the contours of medical negligence law in India. Together they establish that the medical profession must be protected from being held liable for outcomes that are not caused by any negligence, while simultaneously reinforcing that genuine negligence - such as performing a sterilisation without ruling out pre-existing pregnancy, or failing to properly occlude the tubes - remains fully actionable.
- The judgment also introduced a public policy dimension to medical negligence law in India: courts must be mindful that automatic liability deters doctors from performing government public health procedures, thereby harming the broader public interest.

MEDLEX360 PRACTICE PEARLS	
What went wrong?	The lower courts presumed negligence solely because pregnancy occurred after sterilisation, without any evidence proving that the surgeon had performed the procedure negligently.
Risk Management Takeaways	• Do not assume liability merely because a sterilisation fails; negligence must be affirmatively established. • Counsel patients that no sterilisation method is 100% effective and explain the recognised risk of natural failure. • Rule out pre-existing pregnancy before performing sterilisation. • Follow standard surgical protocols to ensure proper occlusion of both fallopian tubes. • Advise patients on the need for follow-up and interim contraception where clinically indicated until the success of the procedure is reasonably assured. • Communicate promptly and appropriately if any intraoperative difficulty or technical limitation occurs. • Maintain clear, contemporaneous records to demonstrate adherence to the accepted standard of care.
Documentation Checklist	• Written informed consent, including counselling on the possibility of natural failure. • Pre-operative assessment and documentation excluding existing pregnancy. • Operative notes recording the sterilisation technique used and confirmation of bilateral tubal occlusion.

MEDLEX360 PRACTICE PEARLS

- Details of any intraoperative complications or deviations from the planned procedure.
- Sterilisation certificate issued after the procedure.
- Post-operative advice, including warning signs, follow-up instructions, and contraceptive advice where necessary.
- Records of any subsequent consultations, pregnancy diagnosis, counselling, and management.

A poor medical outcome alone does not establish negligence - legal liability arises only when the outcome is shown to have resulted from a breach of the required standard of care.

15. Asha Jaiswal

Full Case Name	Bombay Hospital and Medical Research Centre v. Asha Jaiswal and Others
Citation / Case Number	(2021) 9 SCC 758 (also reported as 2021 INSC 801).
Court / Forum	Supreme Court of India
Date of Judgment	30 November 2021
State / Jurisdiction	Maharashtra (Mumbai)
Type of Case	Civil / Consumer Protection

Background & Facts

A patient was admitted to Bombay Hospital, Mumbai, with gangrene in the lower limbs. The treating vascular surgeon was abroad and unavailable for an extended period - from 9 May 1998 to 7 June 1998 - during which the patient's condition progressively worsened. The surgeon who was physically present failed to consult a vascular specialist in a timely manner, and by the time the specialist was consulted, amputation - though delayed - was performed but proved insufficient to save the patient's life. The State Consumer Commission, applying the doctrine of res ipsa loquitur, had found negligence. The matter reached the Supreme Court on the question of negligence and the application of res ipsa loquitur.

Issues Raised

Whether the delay in consulting a specialist for a patient with a deteriorating gangrenous condition amounts to negligence. When and how does the doctrine of res ipsa loquitur apply in medical negligence cases in India.

Arguments - Complainant / Appellant

The complainant argued that the treating surgeon's prolonged absence and the failure of the available doctors to promptly consult a vascular surgeon when the patient's gangrene was worsening was a clear case of negligence. The deterioration was directly attributable to medical inaction.

Arguments - Respondent

The hospital argued that the treating doctor was not absent without arrangement, that the available medical staff exercised their clinical judgment, and that the condition of the patient made the outcome inevitable. It was argued that res ipsa loquitur should not be applied in medical cases.

Judgment & Ruling

The Supreme Court upheld the finding of negligence. The Court comprehensively discussed the doctrine of res ipsa loquitur in the context of medical negligence and held that it is applicable when: (a) the events giving rise to the accident were within the control of the defendant; (b) the outcome is of a kind that would not ordinarily occur in the absence of negligence; and (c) the defendant has not offered an adequate explanation. The Court emphasised that while the mere unavailability of an operation theatre does not constitute negligence per se, unjustified delay in seeking specialist consultation for a critical condition does.

Key Holdings:

- Medical negligence was not proved against the hospital or doctor on the facts of the case.
- Death of a patient or unsuccessful treatment does not by itself establish negligence.

- Doctors are required to provide reasonable care, not guarantee recovery or survival.
- Res ipsa loquitur cannot be applied mechanically in medical negligence cases without proof of breach of duty.
- The patient was already in a critical condition; deterioration despite treatment did not establish negligence.
- Expert evidence and medical records are important for proving negligence; mere allegations are insufficient.
- The hospital was not negligent merely because certain facilities were unavailable or delayed in the circumstances of the case.
- The Supreme Court set aside the NCDRC's compensation award and dismissed the complaint.

Compensation / Outcome

The Supreme Court allowed the appeals filed by Bombay Hospital and Dr. C. Anand Somaya, set aside the National Consumer Disputes Redressal Commission's order awarding ₹14,18,491 with 9% interest, and dismissed the complaint. The Court held that the complainants had failed to establish medical negligence through expert evidence and that the patient's critical pre-existing condition, rather than any deficiency in treatment, led to his death. The interim amount of ₹5 lakh already released to the complainants pursuant to an earlier order of the Court was not directed to be recovered.

Significance & Impact

The judgment reaffirmed that medical negligence cannot be inferred merely because treatment was unsuccessful or the patient died. It emphasised that negligence must be proved through cogent evidence, ordinarily including expert medical opinion, and cautioned against the routine application of the doctrine of *res ipsa loquitur* in complex medical cases. The decision strengthened the principle that doctors and hospitals are liable only when they fail to exercise the standard of reasonable medical care, thereby reinforcing the burden of proof in medical negligence claims.

KEY LEGAL PRINCIPLES / RATIO DECIDENDI

- The doctrine of res ipsa loquitur (the thing speaks for itself) is applicable in medical negligence cases where the facts, without more, clearly and unambiguously point to negligence.
- For res ipsa loquitur to apply: the occurrence must be of a type not ordinarily happening absent negligence; the thing or process causing the harm must be under the control of the defendant; and the defendant must have no adequate explanation.
- Prolonged absence of a treating doctor without adequate substitute care or specialist referral in a deteriorating case may constitute negligence.
- Mere non-availability of infrastructure is different from an unjustified failure to access available specialist resources.
- Contemporaneous medical records are critical; gaps in records may support an inference of negligence.

MEDLEX360 PRACTICE PEARLS	
What went wrong?	The patient's worsening gangrene was not referred to a vascular specialist in a timely manner despite clinical deterioration, resulting in delayed treatment and death.
Risk Management Takeaways	• Ensure timely specialist consultation or referral when a patient's condition deteriorates beyond the treating physician's expertise.

MEDLEX360 PRACTICE PEARLS	
	• Arrange appropriate substitute care whenever the primary treating doctor is unavailable. • Escalate critical cases promptly and avoid delays in definitive management. • Establish clear referral and escalation protocols for high-risk patients. • Maintain end-to-end contemporaneous medical records to support clinical decision-making. • Recognize that unexplained delays in providing appropriate specialist care may constitute medical negligence.
Documentation Checklist	• Initial assessment and diagnosis with severity of the condition. • Daily clinical progress notes documenting deterioration or improvement. • Records of specialist consultation requests, referrals, and response times. • Documentation of the treating physician's absence and alternate care arrangements. • Clinical rationale for treatment decisions and any delays. • Operative notes, consent forms, and post-operative records where applicable. • Complete nursing notes, vital signs, and communication records with the patient and family.

Prompt referral and timely specialist intervention are essential, as avoidable delays in critical care can amount to medical negligence.

16. Smt. Santra

Full Case Name	State of Haryana v. Smt. Santra
Citation / Case Number	(2000) 5 SCC 182
Court / Forum	Supreme Court of India
Date of Judgment	24 April 2000
State / Jurisdiction	Haryana
Type of Case	Civil

Background & Facts

The respondent, Smt. Santra, underwent a tubectomy (sterilisation) operation at a government hospital in Haryana. Despite the procedure, she conceived and gave birth to a child. She filed a civil suit claiming damages for the failed sterilisation and the cost of raising the unwanted child.

Issues Raised

- Whether failure of a sterilisation operation constitutes medical negligence?
- Can damages be claimed for birth of a child following failed sterilisation?
- What quantum of damages is appropriate in "wrongful conception" cases?

Arguments - Complainant / Appellant

- Sterilisation has a known failure rate.
- Birth of a child cannot be treated as "damage."
- The State cannot be liable for natural physiological events.

Arguments - Respondent

- The surgery was negligently performed.
- She is entitled to damages for unwanted pregnancy and childbirth.
- Additional child has imposed financial burden.

Judgment & Ruling

The Supreme Court dismissed the State's appeal and upheld the award of compensation to Smt. Santra, holding that the failure of a sterilisation operation caused by medical negligence entitled the patient to damages. The Court found that the operating surgeon had negligently failed to occlude one of the respondent's fallopian tubes, resulting in an unwanted pregnancy and the birth of a child. It held that the State was vicariously liable for the negligence of its doctors employed in government hospitals.

The Court further observed that the legal obligation of parents to maintain their child does not extinguish their right to claim compensation for the additional financial burden arising from a negligently performed sterilisation procedure. Accordingly, the decree awarding damages for medical negligence was affirmed.

Key Holdings:

- Wrongful Conception Recognised:
- A cause of action exists where sterilisation fails due to negligence (not merely due to known failure rates).
- Damages Awarded: Compensation was granted for:
    - Pain and suffering of pregnancy and childbirth
    - Medical expenses
    - A sum representing partial cost of raising the child
- No Damages for Child's Birth Per Se: The Court did not treat the child's existence as damage but recognised the economic consequences of the unplanned pregnancy.

- Government Liability: The State, as the employer of government hospital doctors, can be held vicariously liable.

Compensation / Outcome

The Supreme Court held the State of Haryana vicariously liable for the negligent performance of a sterilisation operation in which only one fallopian tube was operated upon despite both requiring sterilisation. The Court upheld the award of compensation to Smt. Santra for the medical negligence that resulted in the birth of an unwanted child, holding that the negligence of the government doctor directly caused the failure of the procedure. It clarified that compensation was for the negligent operation and its consequences, not merely for the birth of the child itself.

Significance & Impact:

State of Haryana v. Smt. Santra is a landmark decision establishing that government hospitals and their medical practitioners can be held liable for negligence in family planning procedures. The judgment distinguished between a sterilisation failure due to natural causes and one caused by negligent performance, emphasizing that the State is vicariously liable for the acts of its employees. It laid the foundation for subsequent sterilisation negligence jurisprudence and was later distinguished in State of Punjab v. Shiv Ram, where the Court held that compensation is not automatic in every sterilisation failure but depends on proof of negligence.

KEY LEGAL PRINCIPLES / RATIO DECIDENDI

- State of Haryana v. Santra recognised "wrongful pregnancy" as actionable in India. It influenced subsequent family planning surgery cases and established State liability for government hospital negligence.

- ➲ A doctor who performs a sterilisation operation without exercising the requisite degree of reasonable skill and care is liable in negligence if the procedure fails due to a negligent act or omission.
- ➲ The mere fact that a sterilisation operation results in pregnancy does not automatically establish negligence. Liability arises only where the failure is attributable to negligent performance of the procedure.
- ➲ The State is vicariously liable for the negligent acts of doctors employed in government hospitals while acting in the course of their official duties.
- ➲ A patient who conceives due to a negligently performed sterilisation operation is entitled to recover compensation for the physical, mental and financial consequences of the unwanted pregnancy.
- ➲ The legal and moral obligation of parents to maintain and care for their child does not extinguish their right to claim damages for the additional burden resulting from medical negligence.
- ➲ Medical professionals undertaking sterilisation procedures owe a duty to perform the operation with reasonable competence and in accordance with accepted medical standards. A breach of this duty giving rise to foreseeable harm constitutes actionable negligence.

MEDLEX360 PRACTICE PEARLS	
What went wrong?	A sterilisation procedure failed, resulting in an unintended pregnancy.
Risk Management Takeaways	• Remember that hospitals are responsible for the systems they create

	• Explain known failure rates before sterilisation procedures • Document counselling regarding residual risk • Obtain procedure-specific informed consent • Follow accepted surgical techniques meticulously • Ensure post-procedure follow-up.
Documentation Checklist	• Sterilisation consent • Counselling records • Follow-up advice

Patients must understand that no procedure offers a 100% guarantee.

17. Achutrao Haribhau Khodwa

Full Case Name	Achutrao Haribhau Khodwa v. State of Maharashtra
Citation / Case Number	(1996) 2 SCC 634; applied post-2000
Court / Forum	Supreme Court of India
Date of Judgment	19 February 1996
State / Jurisdiction	Maharashtra
Type of Case	Civil

Background & Facts

The appellant's wife was admitted to a government hospital for delivery. After a caesarean section, a mop (surgical gauze) was negligently left inside her abdomen. She developed severe complications over the following months, required further surgery to remove the mop, and ultimately died.

Issues Raised

- Whether leaving a foreign object inside a patient's body constitutes negligence per se?
- What is the State's liability for negligence in government hospitals?

Arguments - Complainant / Appellant

- Leaving a mop inside the patient was clear negligence.
- The subsequent suffering and death were directly caused by the error.

Arguments - Respondent

- The surgical team followed standard procedures.

- The complication was unfortunate but not attributable to specific negligence.

Judgment & Ruling

The Supreme Court of India held that a hospital and its doctors can be held liable for medical negligence when a patient suffers injury due to a failure to exercise reasonable skill and care expected of competent medical professionals. The Court observed that doctors are not liable merely because a treatment fails, but only when their conduct falls below the accepted standard of medical practice. In this case, a surgical mop was negligently left inside the patient's body after an operation, causing serious complications. The Court ruled that such negligence clearly established the hospital's liability and awarded compensation to the patient's family. The judgment reaffirmed that healthcare professionals owe a duty of care to patients and may be held accountable for avoidable acts of negligence.

Key Holdings:

- **Res Ipsa Loquitur:** Leaving a foreign object in a patient's body speaks for itself as negligence. The burden shifts to the defendant to explain.
- **Sovereign Immunity Rejected:** The State cannot claim sovereign immunity for tortious acts in hospitals. Government hospitals are liable for employee negligence.
- **Compensation:** ₹1,50,000 was awarded as compensation.

Compensation / Outcome

The Supreme Court upheld the finding of medical negligence against the government hospital after a surgical mop was negligently left inside the patient’s abdomen during a sterilisation operation, leading to severe complications and her eventual death.

The Court held the State of Maharashtra vicariously liable for the negligence of its hospital staff and affirmed the award of compensation to the deceased patient's legal representatives.

Significance & Impact:

Achutrao Haribhau Khodwa v. State of Maharashtra is a landmark judgment on medical negligence that reaffirmed the State's vicarious liability for negligent acts committed by doctors and hospital staff in government hospitals. The Court emphasised that leaving a foreign object inside a patient after surgery is a clear instance of negligence and that hospitals owe patients a duty to maintain reasonable standards of care. The decision remains an important precedent on hospital liability and the accountability of public healthcare institutions for preventable medical errors.

KEY LEGAL PRINCIPLES / RATIO DECIDENDI

- This case is foundational for claims involving foreign objects left during surgery. It established that such cases are amenable to the doctrine of res ipsa loquitur and confirmed State liability for government hospital negligence

MEDLEX360 PRACTICE PEARLS	
What went wrong?	A surgical mop was left inside the patient's abdomen, resulting in severe complications and death.
Risk Management Takeaways	• Remember that hospitals are responsible for the systems they create • Follow surgical count protocols without exception

MEDLEX360 PRACTICE PEARLS	
	• Conduct final verification before wound closure • Empower theatre staff to speak up • Use surgical safety checklists • Investigate count discrepancies immediately
Documentation Checklist	• Instrument count records • Sponge count records • Operative notes

Nothing should remain inside a patient except what was intentionally placed there.

18. Spring Meadows Hospital

Full Case Name	Spring Meadows Hospital v. Harjol Ahluwalia
Citation / Case Number	(1998) 4 SCC 39; applied post-2000
Court / Forum	Supreme Court of India
Date of Judgment	25 March 1998
State / Jurisdiction	Pan-India
Type of Case	Consumer Protection

Background & Facts

A seven-year-old child was admitted for a minor surgical procedure requiring general anaesthesia. Due to negligent administration of anaesthesia and failure to properly monitor, the child suffered cardiac arrest and severe brain damage, resulting in permanent disability (effectively a vegetative state).

Issues Raised

- Whether the hospital and anaesthetist were negligent?
- Who can claim compensation - the patient and/or the parents?
- What quantum of compensation is appropriate for permanent vegetative disability?

Arguments - Complainant / Appellant

- Monitoring was inadequate.
- The child will require lifelong care at enormous cost.
- Parents suffered emotional and financial devastation.

Arguments - Respondent

- Standard aesthetic protocols were followed.
- The reaction was unforeseeable.

Judgment & Ruling

The Supreme Court of India held that hospitals and medical professionals are liable for negligence when their actions fall below the standard of reasonable medical care, and compensation may be awarded not only to the patient but also to affected family members. In this case, a child suffered permanent brain damage after being administered the wrong injection due to the negligence of hospital staff. The Court found both the hospital and the attending doctor liable for the negligent treatment. It also recognised that the parents, as consumers of medical services, were entitled to compensation for the mental agony and suffering caused by the negligence.

Key Holdings:

- **Vicarious Liability of Hospitals:**
  Hospitals are vicariously liable for the negligence of staff, including anaesthetists, whether employed or on contract.
- **Dual Compensation:**
  Both the injured patient and the parents are entitled to compensation - the child for the injury, the parents for their own suffering and the burden of care.
- **Significant Compensation:**
  ₹12.5 lakhs was awarded (substantial for the time), with a breakdown for the child's care and parents' suffering.

Compensation / Outcome

The Supreme Court held *Spring Meadows Hospital* and the attending doctor liable for gross medical negligence after a nurse administered the wrong injection to a minor child, causing irreversible brain damage. The Court upheld the award of compensation to the child and also recognised the parents as consumers under the Consumer Protection Act, entitling them to separate compensation for the mental agony, trauma, and financial burden they suffered as a result of the hospital's negligence.

Significance & Impact:

Spring Meadows Hospital v. Harjol Ahluwalia is a landmark decision that broadened the scope of medical negligence and consumer protection jurisprudence in India. The Court affirmed that hospitals are vicariously liable for the negligent acts of their employees, including nurses, and recognised that the parents of an injured patient may also claim compensation as consumers. The judgment significantly strengthened patient rights and established an important precedent for awarding damages in cases involving catastrophic medical negligence and lifelong disability.

KEY LEGAL PRINCIPLES / RATIO DECIDENDI

- Spring Meadows is frequently cited for establishing hospitals' vicarious liability for all staff actions during treatment. It also recognised parents' independent right to compensation for a child's injury, which has been followed in subsequent paediatric negligence cases.

MEDLEX360 PRACTICE PEARLS	
What went wrong?	A child suffered permanent brain damage because of negligent administration of anaesthesia and inadequate intraoperative monitoring.

MEDLEX360 PRACTICE PEARLS	
Risk Management Takeaways	• Adhere strictly to accepted anaesthesia protocols before, during, and after surgery. • Continuously monitor the patient's vital parameters throughout anaesthesia and respond immediately to any deterioration. • Ensure trained anaesthesia personnel and fully functional resuscitation equipment are available at all times. • Clearly define and enforce staff responsibilities, recognizing that hospitals are vicariously liable for the acts of their healthcare providers. • Conduct regular training, simulation drills, and audits to strengthen patient safety during anaesthesia.
Documentation Checklist	• Pre-anaesthetic assessment and fitness evaluation. • Informed consent for anaesthesia and the surgical procedure. • Anaesthesia record detailing drugs, dosages, airway management, and timing. • Continuous intraoperative monitoring charts (pulse, blood pressure, oxygen saturation, ECG, etc.). • Documentation of any adverse events and resuscitative measures undertaken. • Post-anaesthesia recovery and monitoring records. • Maintenance and readiness records of anaesthesia and resuscitation equipment.

Meticulous anaesthesia care and continuous monitoring are essential, as preventable lapses can cause lifelong harm and expose both the clinician and the hospital to liability.

19. Savita Garg

Full Case Name	Savita Garg v. Director, National Heart Institute
Citation / Case Number	(2004) 8 SCC 56
Court / Forum	Supreme Court of India
Date of Judgment	5 November 2004
State / Jurisdiction	New Delhi
Type of Case	Consumer Protection

Background & Facts

The appellant's husband underwent coronary bypass surgery at the National Heart Institute, New Delhi. Post-operatively, a surgical mop was discovered left inside his chest cavity. He developed severe septicemia and died shortly thereafter. The widow filed a consumer complaint alleging gross negligence.

Issues Raised

- Whether leaving a mop constitutes actionable negligence?
- What compensation is appropriate when death results?

Arguments - Complainant / Appellant

- The mop left inside directly caused infection and death.
- This is a clear case of res ipsa loquitur.

Arguments - Respondent

- Multiple surgeries were performed, and the mop may have been left during a later procedure.
- All reasonable care was exercised

Judgment & Ruling

The Supreme Court of India held that once a patient establishes a prima facie case of medical negligence, the burden shifts to the hospital and treating doctors to explain that proper care and accepted medical standards were followed. The Court observed that patients and their families often lack access to medical records and technical knowledge, making it difficult for them to prove negligence. It ruled that hospitals cannot avoid liability by withholding relevant information or failing to produce evidence regarding the treatment provided. The judgment emphasised transparency, accountability, and the duty of hospitals to maintain and disclose medical records when required.

Key Holdings:

- **Clear Negligence:**
  Leaving a foreign body inside a patient is inexcusable negligence. The doctrine of res ipsa loquitur applies.
- **Hospital's Responsibility:**
  The hospital is responsible for ensuring surgical counts are complete
- **Compensation:**
  ₹25 lakhs were awarded - a significant amount reflecting the earning capacity of the deceased and the family's loss

Compensation / Outcome

The Supreme Court set aside the order dismissing the complaint and restored the consumer proceedings, holding that the complainant was entitled to pursue her claim for medical negligence against the hospital. The Court ruled that once a patient establishes a prima facie case, the burden shifts to the hospital and treating doctors—who possess the relevant medical records and knowledge—to explain that there was no negligence. The matter was remitted for adjudication on merits rather than being dismissed for non-impleadment of the treating doctor.

Significance & Impact:

Savita Garg v. Director, National Heart Institute is a significant decision on the evidentiary burden in medical negligence cases. The Supreme Court held that hospitals cannot avoid liability merely because the treating doctor is not impleaded and emphasised that medical institutions, being in possession of the relevant records and expertise, must adequately explain the treatment provided once a prima facie case is made out. The judgment strengthened patients' access to remedies under consumer law by reducing procedural hurdles and reinforcing hospital accountability.

KEY LEGAL PRINCIPLES / RATIO DECIDENDI

- This case reinforced the principles from Achutrao Khodwa and established higher compensation standards for deaths arising from retained foreign objects.
- While the complainant must establish a prima facie case of medical negligence, the burden shifts to the hospital or treating doctors to explain the course of treatment once the relevant medical facts and records are exclusively within their knowledge.
- Hospitals are under a duty to maintain proper medical records and produce them before the adjudicating forum. Failure to produce records or to explain the treatment may justify an adverse inference against the hospital.
- A hospital cannot evade liability by contending that every doctor involved in the treatment has not been impleaded. Where negligence is alleged against treatment provided by the hospital, it is for the hospital to disclose the identity and role of the medical professionals concerned and defend the treatment administered.

- Proceedings before consumer forums are intended to provide an accessible and effective remedy. Technical procedural objections, including non-joinder of individual doctors, should not defeat a bona fide claim where the hospital is a party to the proceedings.
- **Doctrine of special knowledge:** Facts relating to diagnosis, treatment and medical management are matters within the special knowledge of the hospital and its doctors. Accordingly, under the principles embodied in Section 106 of the Indian Evidence Act, the hospital bears the responsibility of explaining those facts when its conduct is questioned.
- The decision reinforces the objective of consumer protection law by ensuring that hospitals remain accountable for the treatment rendered within their institutions and that patients are not denied effective redress because they lack access to technical medical information or the identity of every treating professional.

MEDLEX360 PRACTICE PEARLS	
What went wrong?	A surgical mop was left inside the patient's chest during surgery, leading to severe infection and death.
Risk Management Takeaways	• Perform standardized surgical counts before incision closure and at the end of every procedure. • Use the WHO Surgical Safety Checklist and enforce strict compliance with count protocols. • Immediately investigate and resolve any count discrepancy before wound closure. • Foster clear communication and accountability among the surgical team.

MEDLEX360 PRACTICE PEARLS	
	• Consider adjunct technologies (e.g., radio-opaque mops or barcode/RFID tracking systems) where available. • Recognize that retained foreign objects are preventable events that may constitute negligence under the doctrine of *res ipsa loquitur*.
Documentation Checklist	• Pre, intra, and post-operative surgical count records. • WHO Surgical Safety Checklist with team sign-offs. • Operative notes documenting completion • Reconciliation of instrument, needle, and sponge counts. • Documentation of any count discrepancies and corrective actions taken. • Use and verification of radio-opaque or tracked surgical sponges, where applicable. • Post-operative monitoring records and documentation of any complications.

Strict adherence to basic surgical safety protocols prevents avoidable harm and protects both patients and healthcare providers.

20. Jaspal Singh

Full Case Name	Postgraduate Institute of Medical Education & Research v. Jaspal Singh & ors.
Citation / Case Number	(2009) 7 SCC 330
Court / Forum	Supreme Court of India
Date of Judgment	17 July 2009
State / Jurisdiction	Punjab
Type of Case	Consumer Protection / Medical Negligence

Background & Facts

A female patient with 50% burn injuries was admitted to PGIMER, Chandigarh - one of India's premier public medical institutions. During the course of her treatment, she was administered a mismatched blood transfusion. The incompatible blood group caused a severe transfusion reaction. The patient died approximately 40 days after the incident. Her family, represented by Jaspal Singh, filed a complaint alleging that the hospital's failure to verify blood compatibility before transfusion was a clear and inexcusable act of negligence.

Issues Raised

- Whether the administration of incompatible blood constituted medical negligence, or whether it fell within the range of acceptable professional error.
- Whether PGIMER, as a premier public institution, could be held liable under consumer protection law.
- What standard of care applies to blood transfusion procedures in a leading teaching hospital.

Arguments - Complainant / Appellant

- PGIMER is a national institution of the highest repute, with complex, high-volume medical operations.
- Managing critically ill burns patients involves multiple simultaneous interventions, and errors in such high-pressure situations may not always indicate negligence.

Arguments - Respondent

- Verification of blood group compatibility before transfusion is a fundamental and non-negotiable protocol - it is not a matter of clinical judgment.
- The patient, already vulnerable due to severe burns, was killed by an error that a basic cross-matching check would have prevented.
- The institution's reputation cannot substitute for adherence to standard safety procedures.

Judgment & Ruling

The Supreme Court of India held that medical professionals and hospitals are liable for negligence when they fail to exercise the reasonable degree of skill and care expected in treating a patient, resulting in avoidable harm. The Court emphasised that while doctors are not insurers of successful treatment, they are expected to adhere to accepted standards of medical practice. In this case, negligence in the patient's treatment led to serious injury, and the Court upheld the award of compensation to the victim. It reaffirmed that government hospitals and medical institutions are equally accountable for negligent acts committed by their staff.

Key Holdings:

- **Wrong Blood Transfusion is Not an Error of Judgment:**
  The Court held that a mismatched transfusion is not the kind of mistake a hospital exercising ordinary care would ever make. It does not fall under the category of professional judgment - it is a systems failure.
- **Premier Institutions Are Not Exempt:**
  The Court rejected the argument that PGIMER's standing as a leading institution should shield it from liability. Reputation imposes a higher duty, not a lower one.
- **Causation Established:**
  The hospital's breach of duty in administering mismatched blood materially contributed to the patient's death, even if other factors related to the burns were also present.
- **Res Ipsa Loquitur Applied:**
  Mismatched transfusion to a burns patient "by itself speaks of negligence" - the error was self-evident and required no elaborate expert analysis to establish fault.

Compensation / Outcome

The Supreme Court dismissed PGIMER's appeal and upheld the consumer fora's finding of medical negligence, holding the hospital liable for transfusing mismatched blood to the patient, which substantially contributed to her deterioration and death. The Court affirmed the award of ₹2,00,000 as compensation and ₹5,000 as costs to the deceased's husband and minor son, and additionally imposed ₹20,000 as costs on PGIMER for the unsuccessful appeal.

Significance & Impact:

Postgraduate Institute of Medical Education & Research v. Jaspal Singh & Ors. is a significant decision reaffirming that transfusion of the wrong blood group constitutes clear medical negligence and a serious deficiency in service. The Court emphasised that hospitals bear a non-delegable duty to ensure proper verification and administration of blood before transfusion and cannot escape liability by attributing the patient's death solely to underlying medical conditions. The judgment strengthened hospital accountability and reinforced the application of consumer protection principles in cases of preventable medical errors.

KEY LEGAL PRINCIPLES / RATIO DECIDENDI

- This case established that blood group verification before transfusion is a non-negotiable standard of care - it is a protocol, not a judgment call. A hospital that administers incompatible blood cannot shelter behind the complexity of the patient's condition or the institution's reputation. The case is frequently cited as an example of res ipsa loquitur in Indian medical negligence law: certain errors are so basic that the very occurrence of the error proves negligence. It also confirmed that premier public medical institutions are "services" under the Consumer Protection Act and fully amenable to consumer forum jurisdiction.

MEDLEX360 PRACTICE PEARLS	
What went wrong?	The hospital administered incompatible blood to the patient by failing to verify blood group compatibility before transfusion.
Risk Management Takeaways	• Treat blood group verification and cross-matching as mandatory, non-negotiable safety protocols.

MEDLEX360 PRACTICE PEARLS	
	• Implement a two-person or barcode-based verification process before every transfusion. • Follow standardized transfusion checklists without exception, regardless of workload or emergency circumstances. • Ensure staff are regularly trained and assessed on transfusion safety protocols. • Encourage a culture where any uncertainty about blood identity or compatibility results in stopping the transfusion until verification is completed. • Recognize that institutional reputation does not reduce the duty of care; it demands stricter adherence to safety standards.
Documentation Checklist	• Verified patient identity before transfusion. • Blood group and cross-match reports. • Blood unit details (blood group, unit number, expiry date, and compatibility confirmation). • Pre-transfusion checklist signed by the responsible personnel. • Date, time, and identity of the staff administering the transfusion. • Baseline and post-transfusion vital signs with monitoring records. • Documentation of any transfusion reaction and the immediate corrective measures taken. • Consent for blood transfusion, where applicable.

Basic safety protocols are never optional - failure to follow them can itself constitute clear evidence of medical negligence.

21. Dr. Harish Kumar Khurana

Full Case Name	Dr. Harish Kumar Khurana v. Joginder Singh
Citation / Case Number	2021 SCC OnLine SC 673
Court / Forum	Supreme Court of India
Date of Judgment	7 September 2021
State / Jurisdiction	Haryana
Type of Case	Consumer Protection / Medical Negligence

Background & Facts

Smt. Jasbeer Kaur was admitted to Sun Flag Hospital, Faridabad, suffering from hydronephrosis - a condition where urine build-up causes kidney swelling. She was diagnosed with a severely damaged right kidney and a stone in the left kidney. Surgical assessment determined that both kidneys could not be operated on simultaneously. It was decided to operate on the less-affected left kidney first.

Both the patient and her husband, Joginder Singh, gave informed consent acknowledging the high-risk nature of the procedure. The first surgery (9 December 1996), during which Dr. Khurana administered anaesthesia using Pentothal Sodium and Scolin followed by an endotracheal intubation with nitrous oxide and oxygen, was successful. The patient recovered well and, as noted in the case sheet, was herself insistent on proceeding to the second surgery for the right kidney.

On 16 December 1996, the second surgery was conducted using the same anaesthetic protocol. This time, however, the patient's blood pressure dropped sharply, her pulse became faint, and cardiac respiratory arrest occurred. She was placed on a Boyle's machine and an automated ventilator, but could not be revived. Smt. Jasbeer Kaur died on the operating table.

Her husband and children filed a complaint before the National Consumer Disputes Redressal Commission (NCDRC), alleging medical negligence by Dr. Khurana (the anaesthetist) and the hospital. The NCDRC found both guilty and directed payment of ₹17 lakh with interest at 9% per annum from the date of filing. Dr. Khurana and the hospital appealed to the Supreme Court.

Issues Raised

- Whether cardiac arrest and death during a second surgery, where the first surgery using identical anaesthetic protocol was uneventful, can by itself constitute medical negligence.
- Whether the NCDRC's finding of negligence was supportable in the absence of qualified expert medical evidence.
- Whether informed consent had been validly obtained for the second surgery.
- Whether res ipsa loquitur could be invoked in a case involving inherently complex surgical risk.

Arguments - Complainant / Appellant

- Full informed consent was obtained from the patient's husband, including acknowledgment of the high-risk nature of the second surgery.
- Cardiac arrest is a known and documented risk during anaesthesia and surgery - its occurrence does not automatically indicate negligence.
- The identical anaesthetic technique had been used successfully in the first surgery days earlier. The NCDRC's reliance on the notation of "poor tolerance to anaesthesia" was misplaced - this had not been a problem during the first procedure.

- The hospital had adequate equipment including a Boyle's machine; the anaesthetist's manual ventilation was appropriate under the circumstances.
- Every adverse surgical outcome cannot and should not be characterised as medical negligence.
- No qualified medical expert had testified before the NCDRC to establish that the standard of care was breached.

Arguments - Respondent

- The case sheet from the first surgery contained a notation by the operating surgeon, Dr. Majumdar, recording the patient's poor tolerance to anaesthesia - this warning was not acted upon before the second surgery.
- The patient was taken for the second surgery too soon after the first, without adequate reassessment of anaesthetic risk.
- A ventilator was not readily available during the emergency; equipment failure contributed to the patient's death.
- The patient's consent for the second surgery was not independently obtained from her.
- After cardiac arrest, there was unacceptable delay in summoning a cardiologist or neurologist, as the doctor had to be located and took time to attend.

Judgment & Ruling

The Supreme Court of India held that a doctor cannot be held liable for medical negligence merely because a treatment has failed or the patient has suffered an adverse outcome. The Court reaffirmed that negligence must be established through credible evidence showing that the doctor's conduct fell below the standard of a reasonably competent medical professional. It emphasised that courts should ordinarily rely on expert medical opinion before concluding that a doctor was negligent, especially in complex medical matters. The judgment reiterated the principles laid down in the Jacob Mathew v. State of Punjab case and cautioned against frivolous or unsupported claims against medical practitioners. It underscored that liability arises only where there is a clear breach of the accepted standard of care that directly causes harm to the patient.

Key Holdings:

- **Death During Surgery Is Not Automatic Proof of Negligence:**
  An unsuccessful surgery or a patient's death on the operating table cannot, by itself, be treated as evidence of medical negligence. Negligence must be separately proved on the facts.
- **Expert Medical Evidence is Indispensable:**
  Where a medical case is complex, adjudicating forums cannot rely on inference, assumption, or lay interpretation of clinical notations. Qualified expert testimony is essential to establish that the standard of care was breached.
- **Res Ipsa Loquitur Does Not Apply Here:**
  The doctrine applies only where negligence is self-evident from the very nature of the event. Given that the first surgery with the identical anaesthetic protocol was uneventful and successful, the mere occurrence of cardiac arrest during the second procedure was not self-evidently negligent.
- **Informed Consent Was Valid:**
  Obtaining the patient's husband's consent for the second surgery, in the context of her own expressed willingness to proceed, was reasonable and adequate.
- **NCDRC's Reasoning Overturned:**
  The NCDRC had relied on a clinical notation about poor anaesthetic tolerance without any expert examination of what that notation actually meant. Such an approach is legally impermissible in complex medical negligence cases.

Compensation / Outcome

The Supreme Court allowed the appeal filed by Dr. Harish Kumar Khurana, set aside the orders of the consumer fora awarding compensation to the complainant, and dismissed the medical negligence complaint. The Court held that negligence had not been proved through credible expert medical evidence and that an adverse medical outcome or unsuccessful treatment, by itself, does not establish negligence.

Significance & Impact:

Dr. Harish Kumar Khurana v. Joginder Singh is an important judgment reaffirming that medical negligence must be established by reliable evidence, ordinarily including expert medical opinion, particularly where the issues involve specialized medical knowledge. The Court cautioned consumer fora against substituting their own views for expert medical judgment and reiterated that doctors are liable only where there is a demonstrable breach of the standard of reasonable medical care, thereby reinforcing the principles laid down in Jacob Mathew v. State of Punjab and subsequent medical negligence jurisprudence.

KEY LEGAL PRINCIPLES / RATIO DECIDENDI

- This case is a cornerstone authority for the proposition that a bad outcome is not the same as negligence. The Supreme Court firmly held that to establish medical negligence, there must be sufficient material or expert medical evidence before the adjudicating authority - courts and consumer forums cannot substitute their own lay assessment of clinical decisions for qualified medical opinion. The case also clarifies the limits of res ipsa loquitur in the medical context: the doctrine applies only where negligence is obvious on the face of the event, not wherever a patient dies. It is widely cited alongside Jacob Mathew v. State of Punjab (2005) 6 SCC 1 as defining the evidentiary threshold in Indian medical negligence litigation.

MEDLEX360 PRACTICE PEARLS	
What went wrong?	The patient's death during the second surgery was wrongly presumed to be due to medical negligence despite the absence of expert evidence establishing any breach of the standard of care.
Risk Management Takeaways	• Liability requires proof of a breach of the standard of care. • Obtain and document informed consent, particularly for high-risk procedures. • Perform and record a thorough pre-operative reassessment before each staged surgery. • Maintain complete anaesthesia and intraoperative monitoring records. • Ensure emergency equipment and resuscitation facilities are functional and readily available. • Seek and preserve expert medical opinions when complex clinical decisions or outcomes are likely to be scrutinized.
Documentation Checklist	• Detailed pre-operative evaluation and risk assessment for each surgery. • Informed consent documenting the nature of the procedure, risks, and alternatives.

	• Anaesthesia records, including drugs administered, dosages, monitoring parameters, and intraoperative events. • Operative notes and perioperative monitoring charts. • Documentation of any intraoperative complications and resuscitative measures undertaken. • Equipment availability and functionality records, where relevant. • Post-event clinical notes and specialist consultations, if obtained.

An adverse medical outcome does not by itself prove negligence - liability must be supported by credible evidence that the accepted standard of care was breached.

22. Dr. Archana Sharma

Full Case Name	Dr. Archana Sharma Matter
Citation / Case Number	Unreported; widely covered 2022
Court / Forum	Various - including Supreme Court observations
Date of Judgment	March 2022 (incident)
State / Jurisdiction	Rajasthan
Type of Case	Criminal (IPC Section 302 charges initially filed)

Background & Facts

Dr. Archana Sharma was a senior gynaecologist practicing at a private hospital in Rajasthan. A pregnant woman in critical condition was referred to her for emergency treatment. Despite timely medical intervention, the patient died due to severe postpartum haemorrhage, a recognised obstetric complication.

Following the patient's death, the deceased's family lodged a police complaint. An FIR was registered under Section 302 of the Indian Penal Code (IPC) alleging murder. The registration of murder charges against a treating doctor triggered widespread concern within the medical community.

Before any arrest took place, Dr. Sharma died by suicide, leaving behind a note expressing distress over the criminal proceedings. Her death led to nationwide protests by doctors and renewed debate regarding the criminal prosecution of medical professionals for adverse clinical outcomes.

Issues Raised

- Whether registration of murder charges (Section 302 IPC) against a doctor for an alleged act of medical negligence is legally sustainable.
- The distinction between civil negligence, criminal negligence, and offences such as murder.
- The need to protect healthcare professionals from arbitrary criminal prosecution while ensuring accountability for genuine medical misconduct.
- Whether existing safeguards laid down by the Supreme Court regarding criminal prosecution of doctors were being properly followed

Subsequent Legal Proceedings

Following Dr. Sharma's death, medical associations and doctors filed writ petitions before the Supreme Court seeking stronger safeguards against arbitrary criminal prosecution of healthcare professionals. These petitions relied primarily on the principles laid down in Jacob Mathew v. State of Punjab (2005), which governs criminal liability for medical negligence.

The Supreme Court did not take Suo motu cognizance of Dr. Sharma's case, nor did it deliver a reported judgment specifically arising out of her death. However, the incident became an important catalyst for renewed discussion on the application of criminal law to medical practice.

Existing Legal Principles

The legal position established by earlier Supreme Court decisions remains that:

- Ordinary medical negligence does not amount to murder.
- Criminal prosecution of doctors requires evidence of gross negligence or recklessness, not merely an adverse medical outcome.

- Before initiating criminal prosecution for alleged medical negligence, investigating authorities should ordinarily obtain an independent and competent medical opinion, consistent with the principles laid down in *Jacob Mathew v. State of Punjab*.

Policy Impact

- The incident prompted nationwide discussions on legal protections for healthcare professionals.
- Medical associations renewed demands for uniform statutory safeguards against frivolous criminal prosecution and violence against healthcare workers.
- The case reinforced awareness among investigating agencies regarding the need to distinguish medical negligence from criminal offences.

SIGNIFICANCE AND PRECEDENTIAL IMPACT

- ➲ Although Dr. Archana Sharma's case did not result in a reported judicial precedent, it became one of the most significant medico-legal incidents in recent years.
- ➲ The case highlighted the consequences of prematurely criminalizing adverse medical outcomes and reinforced the importance of adhering to the safeguards established by the Supreme Court in *Jacob Mathew v. State of Punjab*.
- ➲ The incident continues to serve as an important case study in medical law, criminal liability, and risk management for healthcare professionals.

MEDLEX360 PRACTICE PEARLS	
What went wrong?	A serious obstetric complication resulted in the registration of an FIR for murder before expert medical evaluation, leading to immense psychological distress for the treating doctor and sparking nationwide concern regarding misuse of criminal law in cases of alleged medical negligence.
Risk Management Takeaways	• Maintain complete records in all high-risk cases • Seek peer support after adverse events • Inform professional indemnity insurers promptly • Cooperate with investigations professionally • Understand legal protections available to doctors • Be familiar with the legal principles governing criminal negligence in medical practice
Documentation Checklist	• Emergency assessment and treatment records • Referral notes and transfer documents • Documentation of counselling provided to the patient's relatives • Expert opinions

An adverse outcome should trigger review, not automatic criminalization

23. Dr. Suresh Gupta

Full Case Name	Dr. Suresh Gupta v. Govt. of NCT of Delhi
Citation / Case Number	(2004) 6 SCC 422
Court / Forum	Supreme Court of India
Date of Judgment	4 August 2004
State / Jurisdiction	Delhi
Type of Case	Criminal

Background & Facts

The appellant, a plastic surgeon, performed a cosmetic surgery (nasal reconstruction) on a patient at Apollo Hospital, Delhi. During the procedure, the patient died of asphyxia. The prosecution alleged that the doctor negligently failed to ensure proper anaesthesia and airway management.

Issues Raised

- What degree of negligence is required for criminal prosecution under Section 304-A IPC?
- Does failing to insert a cuffed endotracheal tube constitute criminal negligence?

Arguments - Complainant / Appellant

- The death resulted from a known aesthetic complication.
- Proper precautions were taken.
- The charge sheet does not disclose criminal negligence.

Arguments - Respondent

- Failure to use a cuffed tube was gross negligence.
- The doctor had duty to ensure airway safety.

Judgment & Ruling

The Supreme Court of India held that a doctor can be held criminally liable for medical negligence only when the negligence is gross or of a very high degree, and not for a mere error of judgment or ordinary negligence. The Court observed that criminal prosecution of doctors should be undertaken with great caution to prevent harassment of medical professionals performing their duties in good faith. It ruled that for an offence under Section 304A of the Indian Penal Code, the prosecution must prove gross negligence or recklessness directly causing the patient's death. The judgment distinguished civil negligence, which may attract compensation, from criminal negligence, which requires a much higher threshold of proof. It sought to balance patient rights with the need to protect doctors from unwarranted criminal proceedings.

Key Holdings:

- **High Threshold for Criminal Negligence:**
  Mere negligence is insufficient. Criminal liability requires gross negligence or recklessness.
- **Distinction Articulated:**
  The Court distinguished between ordinary negligence (civil liability) and gross negligence (criminal liability).
- **No Criminal Case Made Out:**
  The charge sheet did not establish the high degree of negligence required for criminal prosecution.

Compensation / Outcome

The Supreme Court quashed the criminal proceedings against Dr. Suresh Gupta, holding that the material on record did not disclose the degree of negligence necessary to constitute the offence of causing death by negligence under Section 304A of the Indian Penal Code. The Court clarified that, while the case did not justify criminal prosecution, it did not preclude the possibility of civil liability or disciplinary action where appropriate.

Significance & Impact:

Dr. Suresh Gupta v. Government of NCT of Delhi is a landmark judgment distinguishing criminal medical negligence from civil negligence. The Court held that criminal liability arises only where the doctor's conduct amounts to gross or reckless negligence, and not for every error of judgment or inadvertent mistake. This decision laid the foundation for the higher threshold for prosecuting medical professionals in criminal cases, a principle later reaffirmed and elaborated in Jacob Mathew v. State of Punjab, thereby protecting doctors from criminal prosecution for ordinary negligence while preserving civil remedies for patients.

KEY LEGAL PRINCIPLES / RATIO DECIDENDI

- Dr. Suresh Gupta was a precursor to Jacob Mathew and helped establish the elevated threshold for criminal medical negligence. It is frequently cited together with Jacob Mathew for criminal medical negligence defences.

MEDLEX360 PRACTICE PEARLS	
What went wrong?	A patient died during surgery, leading to criminal negligence allegations.
Risk Management Takeaways	• Understand the distinction between civil and criminal negligence • Follow anaesthesia and airway protocols rigorously • Maintain complete perioperative records • Preserve evidence in serious incidents • Obtain expert review when required.
Documentation Checklist	• Anaesthesia records • Operative notes • Monitoring charts

Criminal negligence requires recklessness, not merely an unfortunate outcome

24. Parmanand Katara

Full Case Name	Parmanand Katara v. Union of India
Citation / Case Number	(1989) 4 SCC 286; principles applied post-2000
Court / Forum	Supreme Court of India
Date of Judgment	28 August 1989
State / Jurisdiction	Pan-India
Type of Case	Public Interest Litigation

Background & Facts

A human rights lawyer highlighted through PIL the problem of accident victims being denied emergency medical treatment by hospitals that feared police formalities. Patients were dying while hospitals awaited police clearance.

Issues Raised

- Do hospitals have a duty to provide emergency treatment regardless of police formalities?
- Can medico-legal formalities override the duty to save life?

Judgment & Ruling

The Supreme Court of India held that every doctor, whether in a government or private hospital, has a legal duty to provide immediate emergency medical treatment to preserve life, without waiting for legal formalities such as police procedures or jurisdictional issues. This judgment strengthened the right to life under Article 21 of the Indian Constitution by prioritizing emergency medical care over procedural requirements. The Court emphasised that preserving human life is of paramount importance and overrides administrative or legal technicalities. It ruled that no hospital or doctor can refuse treatment to an accident victim on the ground that the case belongs to another hospital or requires police clearance. The decision laid the foundation for emergency medical care as a legal obligation across India. It has been widely relied upon in later cases concerning patients' rights and access to urgent healthcare. This landmark judgment continues to guide hospitals and medical professionals in fulfilling their duty to save lives first.

Key Holdings:

- **Duty to Treat Emergencies:**
  Every doctor and hospital has a professional and legal obligation to provide emergency medical care to stabilize and save patients' lives.
- **Police Formalities Secondary:**
  Medical treatment cannot be delayed pending police formalities, completion of FIRs, or identification of the patient.
- **Article 21 Invoked:**
  The right to emergency medical care was linked to the right to life under Article 21 of the Constitution.
- **Directions Issued:**
  - Hospitals must treat road accident victims immediately.
  - Police formalities can follow after patient is stabilized.
  - No prosecution for doctors/hospitals providing emergency care in good faith.

Compensation / Outcome

The Supreme Court did not award monetary compensation but issued binding directions that every doctor, whether in a government or private hospital, has a professional obligation to provide immediate emergency medical treatment to preserve life without waiting for police formalities or medico-legal procedures.

The Court directed that procedural requirements must not delay urgent treatment, thereby placing the preservation of human life above all other considerations.

Significance & Impact:

Parmanand Katara v. Union of India is a landmark judgment that established the right to emergency medical care as an integral part of the right to life under Article 21 of the Constitution. The Court held that the duty to save human life overrides procedural and jurisdictional concerns, ensuring that accident victims receive prompt treatment regardless of the nature of the hospital. The decision has had a lasting impact on emergency healthcare in India and remains a foundational precedent governing the legal and ethical obligations of medical professionals to provide immediate lifesaving care.

SIGNIFICANCE AND PRECEDENTIAL VALUE

- Parmanand Katara established the fundamental duty of emergency care and removed legal obstacles to treating accident victims. The principles were codified in subsequent legislation (Motor Vehicles Act amendments, Good Samaritan guidelines) and remain foundational to emergency medicine law in India.

MEDLEX360 PRACTICE PEARLS	
What went wrong?	Emergency patients were being denied timely treatment due to police and administrative formalities.

MEDLEX360 PRACTICE PEARLS	
Risk Management Takeaways	• Understand the distinction between civil and criminal negligence • Stabilize first, document later • Never wait for police clearance • Train emergency staff regularly • Establish emergency treatment protocols • Treat every emergency as time-sensitive.
Documentation Checklist	• Time of arrival • • Stabilization measures • Referral records

Saving life always comes before paperwork

25. Common Cause Case (Passive Euthanasia)

Full Case Name	Common Cause v. Union of India (Passive Euthanasia)
Citation / Case Number	(2018) 5 SCC 1
Court / Forum	Supreme Court of India (Constitutional Bench)
Date of Judgment	9 March 2018
State / Jurisdiction	Pan-India
Type of Case	Constitutional / Civil

Background & Facts

The NGO Common Cause filed a public interest litigation seeking recognition of an individual's right to die with dignity, including the right to execute a "living will" or advance directive refusing medical treatment in terminal conditions.

Issues Raised

- Does the right to life under Article 21 include the right to die with dignity?
- Is passive euthanasia (withdrawal of life support) permissible in India?
- Can individuals execute legally binding advance directives (living wills)?

Arguments - Complainant / Appellant

- Personal autonomy includes the right to refuse treatment.
- Prolonging life artificially in terminal cases violates dignity.

- Other countries recognize living wills; India should follow.

Arguments - Respondent

Did not oppose the petition but sought guidelines to prevent misuse.

Judgment & Ruling

The Constitution Bench delivered a landmark judgment recognizing passive euthanasia and living wills. It held that the right to die with dignity is an integral part of the right to life under Article 21 of the Constitution, and recognised the legality of passive euthanasia under strict safeguards. The Court permitted the withdrawal or withholding of life-sustaining treatment for terminally ill patients in appropriate circumstances. It also recognised the validity of living wills (advance medical directives), allowing individuals to express their wishes regarding end-of-life medical treatment in advance. The judgment laid down detailed procedural safeguards to prevent misuse, including medical board approvals and judicial oversight (later simplified in subsequent rulings). It emphasised that the patient's autonomy, dignity, and informed consent must be respected in end-of-life decisions. This landmark judgment significantly advanced the recognition of patients' rights and medical ethics in India.

Key Holdings:

- **Right to Die with Dignity Recognised:** The right to life under Article 21 includes the right to die with dignity. Patients in irreversible vegetative states or terminal conditions can have life support withdrawn.
- **Passive Euthanasia Permitted:** Withdrawal of life-sustaining treatment (passive euthanasia) is lawful under strict guidelines. Active euthanasia (affirmative act to cause death) remains prohibited.

- **Advance Directives (Living Wills) Recognised:**
  - An adult of sound mind can execute a living will specifying refusal of treatment in terminal conditions.
  - The directive comes into effect when the patient becomes incapable of decision-making.
- **Detailed Guidelines:** The Court prescribed elaborate guidelines including:
  - Requirements for valid living wills (witnesses, format, storage)
  - Hospital ethics committee review
  - Judicial oversight through the Collector/JMFC
  - Medical board certification of terminal condition
- **Aruna Shanbaug Distinguished:** The earlier judgment (*Aruna Ramchandra Shanbaug v. Union of India*, 2011) permitted passive euthanasia under High Court supervision. This judgment streamlined the process with guidelines.

Compensation / Outcome

The Supreme Court did not award compensation in *Common Cause v. Union of India* but recognised the legality of passive euthanasia and the right of a person to refuse medical treatment under the framework of Article 21 (right to life and personal liberty). The Court permitted the execution of advance medical directives (living wills) and laid down procedural safeguards for withdrawing life-sustaining treatment from terminally ill or permanently incapacitated patients. The earlier guidelines were later modified to simplify the process and make implementation more practical.

Significance & Impact:

Common Cause v. Union of India is a landmark constitutional decision that recognised the right to die with dignity as part of the right to life under Article 21. The judgment distinguished passive euthanasia (withholding or withdrawing life support) from active euthanasia and affirmed patient autonomy in end-of-life medical decisions. It significantly influenced medical ethics and healthcare law in India by establishing a legal framework for advance directives, while balancing individual dignity with safeguards against misuse.

KEY LEGAL PRINCIPLES / RATIO DECIDENDI

➲ Common Cause is a defining medico-legal judgment recognizing patient autonomy and end-of-life rights. It fundamentally changed the legal framework for terminal care and gave patients the right to refuse medical intervention.

MEDLEX360 PRACTICE PEARLS	
What went wrong?	The case addressed uncertainty regarding end-of-life decision-making and patient autonomy.
Risk Management Takeaways	• Respect patient autonomy • Understand living will requirements • Document end-of-life discussions thoroughly • Involve ethics committees where necessary • Follow legal protocols meticulously
Documentation Checklist	• Advance directives • Family discussions • Ethics committee records

Patient autonomy continues even when cure is no longer possible.

26. Aruna Shanbaug

Full Case Name	Aruna Ramachandra Shanbaug v. Union of India & Ors.
Citation / Case Number	(2011) 4 SCC 454
Court / Forum	Supreme Court of India
Date of Judgment	7 March 2011
State / Jurisdiction	Maharashtra / Pan India
Type of Case	Constitutional Law

Background & Facts

Aruna Ramachandra Shanbaug was a nurse working at the King Edward Memorial Hospital in Mumbai. In November 1973, she was brutally assaulted by a hospital employee, resulting in severe brain damage due to prolonged deprivation of oxygen. She remained in a persistent vegetative state (PVS) for nearly 37 years and was cared for continuously by the nursing staff of KEM Hospital.

Journalist and author Pinki Virani filed a writ petition under Article 32 of the Constitution seeking permission for withdrawal of life support and what was popularly described as "mercy killing" for Aruna Shanbaug. The petition raised fundamental questions concerning euthanasia, the right to life, human dignity, and end-of-life medical decision-making.

Issues Raised

- Whether the Constitution recognizes a right to die with dignity as part of Article 21.
- Whether euthanasia is legally permissible in India.
- Whether passive euthanasia and active euthanasia should be treated differently under law.

- Who may make decisions on behalf of a patient in a persistent vegetative state.
- What safeguards should govern withdrawal of life-sustaining treatment.

Arguments - Petitioner

The petitioner argued that Aruna Shanbaug had remained in an irreversible vegetative state for decades without any realistic prospect of recovery. It was contended that continued artificial maintenance of biological existence served no meaningful purpose and that dignity required allowing a peaceful death.

The petitioner further argued that the right to life under Article 21 includes the right to die with dignity in exceptional circumstances involving irreversible suffering and loss of consciousness.

Arguments - Respondents

The State opposed legalization of euthanasia and argued that any such policy decision should be made by Parliament rather than the judiciary.

The staff and nurses of KEM Hospital opposed withdrawal of treatment and asserted that they had cared for Aruna for decades and wished to continue doing so. They maintained that Aruna was not brain dead and that they regarded her as a member of their hospital family.

Judgment & Ruling

The Supreme Court delivered a landmark judgment that fundamentally changed Indian medico-legal jurisprudence.

The Court distinguished between:

- Active euthanasia - deliberate administration of a lethal substance to cause death.
- Passive euthanasia - withdrawal or withholding of life-sustaining medical treatment allowing natural death.

Key Holdings:

- The Court held that active euthanasia remained illegal in India. However, passive euthanasia could be permitted under exceptional circumstances and subject to strict judicial safeguards.
- The Court laid down interim guidelines that would operate until Parliament enacted legislation on the subject.
- Importantly, the Court rejected the specific plea for withdrawal of treatment in Aruna Shanbaug's own case. The Court held that the KEM Hospital staff constituted her true "next friends" and that they wished to continue caring for her. Therefore, no withdrawal of treatment was ordered.

Compensation / Outcome

The Supreme Court did not award compensation in *Aruna Ramachandra Shanbaug v. Union of India & Ors.* Instead, it considered a petition seeking permission for withdrawal of life support from Aruna Shanbaug, who had been in a persistent vegetative state for decades. The Court declined to permit euthanasia in her case after obtaining medical opinions that she was not brain-dead and appeared to have some level of awareness. However, it allowed **passive euthanasia in exceptional cases** and laid down procedural guidelines requiring approval from the High Court before withdrawing life-sustaining treatment.

Significance & Impact:

Aruna Ramachandra Shanbaug v. Union of India & Ors. was a landmark judgment that, for the first time, recognised **passive euthanasia as legally permissible in India** under limited circumstances. The Court distinguished between active and passive euthanasia and emphasised the importance of dignity, medical ethics, and judicial oversight in end-of-life decisions. The guidelines framed in this case governed passive euthanasia matters until they were replaced and modified by the constitutional bench decision in Common Cause v. Union of India, which recognised the right to die with dignity and permitted advance medical directives.

For doctors, intensivists, neurologists, palliative care specialists, and hospital administrators, Aruna Shanbaug remains the foundational Indian case governing end-of-life decision-making.

KEY LEGAL PRINCIPLES / RATIO DECIDENDI

- The Supreme Court delivered a landmark judgment that fundamentally changed Indian medico-legal jurisprudence.
- The Court distinguished between:
- Active euthanasia - deliberate administration of a lethal substance to cause death.
- Passive euthanasia - withdrawal or withholding of life-sustaining medical treatment allowing natural death.
- The Court held that active euthanasia remained illegal in India. However, passive euthanasia could be permitted under exceptional circumstances and subject to strict judicial safeguards. The Court laid down interim guidelines that would operate until Parliament enacted legislation on the subject.
- Importantly, the Court rejected the specific plea for withdrawal of treatment in Aruna Shanbaug's own case. The Court held that the KEM Hospital staff constituted her true “next friends” and that they wished to continue caring for her. Therefore, no withdrawal of treatment was ordered.

MEDLEX360 PRACTICE PEARLS	
What changed?	For the first time, passive euthanasia received judicial recognition in India under carefully controlled conditions.
Risk Management Takeaways	• Withdrawal of life support is a legal decision as well as a medical one. • Documentation of prognosis and neurological status is critical. • Independent expert medical opinions should be obtained. • Family discussions must be carefully recorded. • Ethical committee review should be considered wherever available. • Court approval requirements must be strictly followed.
Documentation Checklist	• Detailed neurological assessments • Brain imaging and specialist reports • Prognosis documentation • Family counselling records • Ethics committee recommendations • Intensive care records • Court orders and legal correspondence

Passive Euthanasia or Living Will is a legally permitted provision.

27. SaveLife Foundation (Good Samaritan Law)

Full Case Name	SaveLife Foundation v. Union of India
Citation / Case Number	Writ Petition (C) No. 235 of 2012
Court / Forum	Supreme Court of India
Date of Judgment	March 30, 2016
State / Jurisdiction	Pan India
Type of Case	Constitutional Writ Petition / Public Interest Litigation (PIL)

Background & Facts

SaveLife Foundation, a non-profit organisation, filed a petition highlighting the plight of accident victims who die due to delays in medical treatment. The case centered on the reluctance of bystanders and Good Samaritans to help accident victims due to:

Issues Raised

- Lack of Legal Protection: Whether Good Samaritans have adequate legal safeguards when assisting accident victims
- Deterrent Effect: Whether fear of legal action discourages citizens from providing emergency aid
- Need for Legislation: Whether statutory protection is required for emergency responders and bystanders
- Constitutional Obligation: Whether the State has a duty to facilitate emergency medical assistance

Arguments - Petitioner

- Good Samaritans face unnecessary legal harassment and criminal prosecution
- Current legal framework creates a chilling effect on voluntary assistance
- Statutory protection is essential to encourage citizen participation in emergency response
- International best practices recognize Good Samaritan protections

Arguments - State

- Existing laws provide adequate framework
- Need for careful investigation to distinguish between genuine help and criminal negligence
- Balancing act between protecting helpers and ensuring accountability

Judgment and Ruling

The Supreme Court of India issued binding guidelines to protect Good Samaritans who help road accident victims from harassment by police and hospitals. The Court recognised that fear of legal and procedural hassles often discourages bystanders from assisting injured persons. It directed that no person assisting an accident victim should be compelled to disclose personal details or be detained unnecessarily. It also mandated that hospitals must provide immediate treatment without insisting on police formalities or payment as a condition for emergency care. The judgment emphasised that saving a human life takes priority over procedural requirements and administrative delays. These guidelines were later incorporated into law by the government, strengthening emergency response and bystander protection in India.

Key Holdings:

- **Good Samaritans must be protected** from harassment while helping road accident victims.
- **No mandatory police involvement:** A Good Samaritan may leave after providing basic information unless they choose to become a witness.
- **Witness examination must be convenient:** Police must examine willing witnesses respectfully and, as far as possible, at their place and time of choice.
- **Identity protection is ensured:** Good Samaritans cannot be discriminated against or unnecessarily compelled to reveal personal details.
- **Affidavit evidence is permitted:** A Good Samaritan may provide evidence through affidavit instead of repeated police/court appearances.
- **Courts should avoid requiring personal appearance** of Good Samaritans unless necessary.
- **Guidelines have binding force:** Supreme Court directions under Articles 32 and 142 are binding until replaced by legislation.

Compensation / Outcome

The Supreme Court approved guidelines issued by the Government of India to protect Good Samaritans who assist road accident victims. The Court ensured that persons helping accident victims would not face unnecessary harassment, repeated questioning, or legal complications, and directed that the guidelines be given statutory force until appropriate legislation was enacted. It also provided for protection of the identity of Good Samaritans and safeguards for those assisting victims during emergencies.

Significance & Impact:

SaveLIFE Foundation v. Union of India is a significant judgment in the field of emergency healthcare and public safety. It strengthened the legal protection available to bystanders who provide immediate assistance to accident victims and promoted the constitutional value of saving human life under Article 21. The decision removed barriers that discouraged people from helping injured persons and contributed to the development of the Good Samaritan framework in India, encouraging timely medical assistance and reducing preventable deaths from road accidents.

SIGNIFICANCE

- ➲ The Good Samaritan law represents the culmination of medico-legal reform protecting both rescuers and emergency healthcare providers. It has increased bystander assistance and reduced barriers to emergency care.
- ➲ The Motor Vehicles (Amendment) Act, 2019, inserted a new section 134A, named "Protection of good Samaritans" which provides that a Good Samaritan shall not be liable for any civil or criminal action for any injury to or death of the victim of an accident.

MEDLEX360 PRACTICE PEARLS	
What went wrong?	The primary issue was the lack of a legal framework to protect individuals who assist accident victims, leading to a reluctance among citizens to provide aid due to fear of legal repercussions.

Risk Management Takeaways	• Importance of clear legal frameworks to encourage citizen participation in emergency situations. • Need for proactive measures by the government to protect Good Samaritans.
Documentation Checklist	• Legal framework documentation for Good Samaritans. • Guidelines for citizens on the rights and protections available under the Good Samaritan Law. • Training and awareness programs for citizens regarding the importance of assisting accident victims

RECENT DEVELOPMENT (2026 UPDATE)

- **SaveLife Foundation & Anr. v. Union of India & Ors., WP(C) No. 726 of 2024, Supreme Court of India, decided 26-27 May 2026**
- A decade after the original 2016 judgment gave India its Good Samaritan Law, SaveLife Foundation returned to the Supreme Court - this time seeking recognition of a broader right to timely trauma care, not merely protection for bystanders who choose to help.

- The Court held that **the right to timely trauma care and emergency medical intervention is itself part of the right to life under Article 21** - extending the reasoning of the 2016 judgment from *protecting those who help* to *guaranteeing that help reaches victims in time*. The Bench emphasised that every minute lost in the "golden hour" after a serious accident can determine survival, and that a robust, responsive trauma-care system is therefore a constitutional obligation, not merely a policy goal.

- Directions issued by the Court include:

  - Full operationalisation of the **PM-RAHAT cashless treatment scheme** for road accident victims within stipulated timelines, including hospital designation, onboarding onto the Transaction Management System, and district-police deployment on the electronic Detailed Accident Report (eDAR) system.
  - **Integration of emergency helpline numbers** into a unified national emergency response number.
  - **Standardisation of ambulance services** and strengthening of trauma-care infrastructure nationwide.
  - Establishment of **trauma registries** to generate data for policy and resource allocation.
  - Continued and strengthened enforcement of the **Good Samaritan protections** first laid down in the 2016 judgment, which had by then also been statutorily codified in the Motor Vehicles (Amendment) Act, 2019.

The 2016 ruling discussed above answered the question "will a bystander who helps be protected?" The 2026 ruling answers the logically connected next question: "will help and the medical system behind it actually arrive in time?"

Read together, the two judgments now form a continuous constitutional thread from bystander protection to systemic emergency-care obligation, both flowing from Article 21.

Hospitals, ambulance operators, and healthcare administrators should expect implementation directions (cashless treatment obligations, eDAR compliance, ambulance standards) to follow in the coming months, and should track compliance requirements as they are notified.

Every rescued patient begins with someone willing to help.

28. M.A. Biviji

Full Case Name	M.A. Biviji v. Sunita & Ors.
Citation / Case Number	2023 INSC 938; Civil Appeal No. 3975 of 2018 (with Civil Appeal No. 4847 of 2018 & Diary No. 21513 of 2018)
Court / Forum	Supreme Court of India
Date of Judgment	19 October 2023
State / Jurisdiction	Pan-India
Type of Case	Civil / Medical Negligence (Consumer Protection)

Background & Facts

The complainant underwent treatment at Suretech Hospital for respiratory complications. During the course of treatment, the treating doctors performed a **Nasotracheal Intubation (NI)** after bronchoscopy. Subsequently, the patient developed permanent respiratory tract deformity and loss of voice. Alleging that these complications resulted from negligent medical management, the complainant approached the National Consumer Disputes Redressal Commission (NCDRC).

The NCDRC held the hospital and the treating doctors liable for medical negligence and awarded compensation. Aggrieved by this decision, the doctors and hospital appealed before the Supreme Court, while the complainant sought enhancement of compensation.

Issues Raised

- Whether the performance of Nasotracheal Intubation constituted medical negligence.

- Whether the complications suffered by the patient were directly attributable to negligent treatment.
- What is the standard for determining negligence against medical professionals.
- Whether an adverse medical outcome by itself establishes negligence.

Judgment & Ruling

The Supreme Court allowed the appeals filed by the doctors and the hospital, set aside the NCDRC's finding of negligence, and dismissed the patient's appeal for enhancement of compensation. The Court held that negligence had not been proved, and reiterated the settled principles governing medical negligence and liability of doctors/hospitals under consumer law. It held that a doctor is not liable merely because treatment has not resulted in a cure or has had an adverse outcome. Liability arises only when there is a failure to exercise reasonable skill and care expected of a competent medical professional. The Court emphasised the importance of expert medical evidence in determining whether the standard of care was breached. It also reinforced that hospitals can be held responsible for the acts of their employees under the principle of vicarious liability. The judgment strengthened the balance between protecting patients' rights and ensuring that doctors are not subjected to unfair claims for genuine medical outcomes.

Key Holdings:

- **Bolam Test Reaffirmed:** A doctor is not negligent merely because another course of treatment might have been preferable. If the treatment adopted is accepted by a responsible body of medical professionals, negligence cannot be inferred.
- **Adverse Outcome Does Not Establish Negligence:** The occurrence of complications or an unsuccessful

treatment outcome is insufficient to impose liability unless there is evidence of breach of the accepted standard of care.

- **Burden of Proof Lies on the Complainant:** Medical negligence must be established through cogent evidence demonstrating breach of duty, causation, and resultant injury. Mere allegations or hindsight cannot substitute proof.
- **Jacob Mathew Principles Reaffirmed:** The Court reiterated that medical professionals are judged differently from ordinary negligence cases. A simple error of judgment or an unsuccessful result does not amount to negligence if the doctor acted in accordance with accepted medical practice.
- **Judicial Deference to Medical Decision-Making:** Courts should avoid substituting their own views for the clinical judgment of qualified medical professionals unless the treatment is shown to be clearly unreasonable or contrary to accepted standards.

Compensation / Outcome

The Supreme Court dismissed the claim for compensation in M.A. Biviji v. Sunita & Ors., holding that medical negligence was not established against the doctors or the hospital. The Court observed that an unsuccessful medical outcome or death of a patient cannot, by itself, be treated as negligence unless there is proof that the medical professionals failed to exercise the required standard of care. The compensation awarded by the lower consumer fora was therefore set aside.

Significance & Impact:

M.A. Biviji v. Sunita & Ors. reaffirmed the principle that doctors cannot be held liable merely because treatment does not result in the desired outcome. The judgment emphasised the need for clear evidence of breach of duty and cautioned against applying hindsight to medical decisions. It strengthened the distinction between an

error of judgment or an adverse result and **actionable medical negligence**, thereby reinforcing the requirement of proving negligence before imposing liability on medical professionals.

SIGNIFICANCE AND PRECEDENTIAL VALUE

- This judgment comprehensively revisits the principles laid down in Jacob Mathew v. State of Punjab and Kusum Sharma v. Batra Hospital, reaffirming that liability cannot be imposed merely because treatment was unsuccessful or complications arose.
- The decision strengthens judicial recognition of the Bolam test, emphasizes evidence-based adjudication, and protects doctors from findings of negligence founded on hindsight rather than accepted medical practice.

MEDLEX360 PRACTICE PEARLS	
What went wrong?	Medical negligence was alleged primarily because the patient developed serious complications after treatment. However, the evidence did not establish that the doctors had departed from accepted medical practice, and the Supreme Court found no breach of the standard of care.
Risk Management Takeaways	• Document the clinical reasoning for significant interventions • Record indications, risks, and alternatives discussed with the patient or relatives

MEDLEX360 PRACTICE PEARLS	
	• Follow recognised clinical guidelines and accepted protocols • Obtain informed consent for invasive procedures wherever applicable • Ensure detailed documentation of complications and subsequent management • Preserve all investigation reports and treatment records for future medico-legal scrutiny
Documentation Checklist	• Complete inpatient treatment records • Procedure notes • Informed consent forms • Investigation reports and imaging • Progress notes and nursing records • Expert opinions, if obtained • Discharge summary and follow-up advice

Medical negligence cannot be inferred merely because treatment fails or complications occur; liability arises only when there is a proven breach of the accepted standard of medical care.

29. V. Krishnakumar (Retinopathy of Prematurity)

Full Case Name	V. Krishnakumar v. State of Tamil Nadu & Ors.
Citation / Case Number	(2015) 9 SCC 388; Civil Appeal No. 8065 of 2009 & Civil Appeal No. 5402 of 2010
Court / Forum	Supreme Court of India
Date of Judgment	1 July 2015 (Doctor's Day)
State / Jurisdiction	Tamil Nadu
Type of Case	Consumer Protection / Medical Negligence / Vicarious Liability

Background & Facts

V. Krishnakumar's wife, Laxmi, was admitted to the Government Hospital for Women and Children, Egmore, Chennai on 30 August 1996. She delivered a premature female infant at 29 weeks of gestation - significantly earlier than the normal term of 38-40 weeks. The newborn, named Sharanya, weighed 1,250 grams and was placed in the intensive care unit (incubator) for 25 days. During this period, she experienced apneic spells (periods of irregular breathing) and was administered supplemental oxygen and blood transfusion - both risk factors for a well-known neonatal complication called Retinopathy of Prematurity (ROP).

The infant was discharged on 23 September 1996. At the time of discharge, the hospital advised the parents to attend post-natal follow-up examinations on Tuesdays. However, the hospital failed to explicitly inform the parents of the risk of ROP or advise them to undergo retinal screening - a mandatory examination for premature infants with birth weight <1500 grams and/or gestational age <32 weeks.

Neither Dr. S. Gopaul (Chief of Neonatology, who also examined the baby at his private clinic when she was 14-15 weeks old) nor Dr. Duraiswamy (the hospital neonatologist) suggested an ophthalmological examination. The parents, trusting that they would be informed of any serious risks, did not seek one independently.

In November 2005 - approximately 9 years after discharge - the mother noticed abnormal visual responses in Sharanya: she appeared unable to focus or follow objects. When an ophthalmological examination was finally conducted, the diagnosis was devastating: ROP Stage 5 in both eyes (total retinal detachment) - the terminal and irreversible stage rendering the child permanently blind. The family pursued a consumer protection complaint, alleging gross medical negligence.

Issues Raised

- Whether the failure to diagnose ROP or advise mandatory retinal screening in a premature infant of high-risk profile constituted medical negligence.
- Whether the hospital and doctors were aware of the risk of ROP in a baby administered supplemental oxygen and blood transfusion.
- Can a hospital cite patient non-compliance with follow-up appointments as a defence when it failed to communicate the specific risk that necessitated the follow-up?
- What is the measure of vicarious liability when both the hospital and individual doctors are negligent?
- How should compensation be calculated for a lifetime of disability caused by preventable blindness?

Arguments - Complainant / Appellant

- It is a well-known medical phenomenon that a premature baby who has been administered supplemental oxygen and blood transfusion is prone to a higher risk of ROP, which can be prevented if detected early.
- The doctors never informed the family of this risk or advised ROP screening despite knowing the baby's high-risk profile.
- Dr. Gopaul, even at the private clinic visit at 14-15 weeks, made no mention of ROP risk - a critical omission.
- The parents acted reasonably: they relied on doctors' expertise and would have sought screening had they been advised of the risk.
- A 9-year delay in diagnosis, rendering the child permanently blind, demonstrates clear breach of the standard of care.

Arguments - Respondent

- The hospital provided standard neonatal care appropriate for 1996 guidelines.
- ROP cannot be detected without specialized ophthalmological examination; clinical suspicion alone is insufficient.
- The hospital advised post-natal follow-up; it was the parents' responsibility to ensure the child attended.
- Not all premature infants develop ROP; the condition's occurrence cannot be predicted with certainty.
- Without expert evidence that the doctors' conduct fell below the standard of care of 1996, negligence cannot be established.

Judgment & Ruling

The Supreme Court of India held that the State and its hospitals can be held liable to pay compensation for death or injury caused due to medical negligence in government healthcare institutions.

The Court observed that failure to provide timely and proper medical care to a patient, especially in emergency or paediatric cases, amounts to a serious breach of duty of care. It emphasised that compensation in such cases must be realistic and not merely symbolic, reflecting the gravity of the loss suffered by the victim's family.

The judgment reinforced that government doctors and hospitals owe a constitutional obligation under Article 21 to protect life with due care and diligence. It also strengthened the principle that public healthcare negligence attracts vicarious liability of the State.

The Supreme Court upheld the finding of medical negligence and awarded a landmark compensation of ₹76 lakh - enhancing the NCDRC's award of ₹5 lakh - finding both the doctors and the State vicariously liable.

This case remains an important precedent on state accountability and compensation in medical negligence matters in India.

Key Holdings:

- **Failure to Advise ROP Screening is Negligence:**
  The disease occurs in infants who are prematurely born and administered oxygen and blood transfusion upon birth, and if detected early enough, it can be prevented. The failure to inform parents of this risk or advise screening constitutes negligence.
- **Standard of Care Includes Communication:**
  A doctor's obligation extends beyond clinical examination - it includes communicating known risks to parents so they

can take informed decisions. Silence about a preventable complication, even if routine follow-up was advised, is negligent.

- **Vicarious Liability of the State and Hospital:**
  The State of Tamil Nadu is vicariously liable for the negligence of its doctors and the institutional failure to establish ROP screening protocols. A government hospital's reputation does not exempt it; it strengthens the duty to provide exemplary care.
- **ROP is Preventable with Early Detection:**
  ROP screening should begin at 31 weeks post-conceptional age or 4 weeks after birth, whichever is later. For infants with birth weight <1500g and gestational age <32 weeks, this is mandatory, not optional.
- **Apportionment of Liability:**
  Both doctors - Dr. Gopaul and Dr. Duraiswamy - are jointly liable. The Chief of Neonatology cannot escape responsibility by examining the child at a private clinic without addressing the ROP risk.
- **Compensation Methodology:**
  The Court adopted the principle of *restitutio in integrum* (restoration to original position as far as possible). Factors included: lifetime care costs, lost wages of parents, pain and suffering, loss of normal life and educational opportunities, and the cost of rehabilitation and assistive devices for a blind child. The State of Tamil Nadu is vicariously liable for the negligence of its doctors and the institutional failure to establish.

Compensation / Outcome

The Supreme Court upheld the liability of the State of Tamil Nadu and the government hospital for medical negligence in the treatment of a child who suffered permanent disability due to improper medical care. The Court enhanced the compensation substantially, awarding **₹1.65 crore** to the victim, considering the lifelong disability, loss of future earning capacity, medical expenses, and the need for continued care and rehabilitation. The Court held that the State was vicariously liable for the negligence of its medical staff.

Significance & Impact:

V. Krishnakumar v. State of Tamil Nadu & Ors. is a landmark judgment on quantification of compensation in medical negligence cases involving permanent disability. The Supreme Court emphasised that compensation must be realistic and must account for the victim's future needs, loss of income, and quality of life rather than being merely symbolic. The decision strengthened the principle that public healthcare institutions can be held accountable for negligence and highlighted the importance of a just, fair, and comprehensive approach to damages in cases of catastrophic medical injury.

KEY LEGAL PRINCIPLES / RATIO DECIDENDI

- This is a landmark judgment establishing that the failure to screen for or advise mandatory screening of a known preventable complication in a high-risk neonatal case constitutes medical negligence, even if the complication is not directly caused by the doctor's clinical intervention.
- The case affirmed that institutional silence - the failure to communicate risks - can be as negligent as active wrongdoing.
- The Supreme Court clarified that guidelines for ROP screening (birth weight <1500g, gestational age <32 weeks) are not aspirational; they are standards of care.
- The judgment also redefined vicarious liability in public hospitals, holding that the State is answerable for systemic failures in protocol and training, not merely individual doctor errors.

- The compensation awarded (₹76 lakh in 2015) set a benchmark for lifetime disability cases and established that preventable blindness in children warrants substantial damages.
- This case is frequently cited alongside Jacob Mathew v. State of Punjab to illustrate the balance between protecting doctors from harassment and holding them to mandatory standards of care in straightforward, guideline-based scenarios.

MEDLEX360 PRACTICE PEARLS	
What went wrong?	The healthcare team failed to inform the parents of the infant's high risk of Retinopathy of Prematurity (ROP) and did not arrange or advise timely mandatory retinal screening, resulting in preventable permanent blindness.
Risk Management Takeaways	• Identify high-risk premature infants and follow established ROP screening guidelines without exception. • Clearly communicate the risk of ROP and the need for timely ophthalmology referral to parents. • Provide written discharge instructions specifying the screening schedule and follow-up requirements. • Ensure referrals are made, documented, and tracked until the patient is evaluated. • Implement standardized neonatal screening protocols and multidisciplinary coordination between neonatologists and ophthalmologists.

MEDLEX360 PRACTICE PEARLS	
Documentation Checklist	• Neonatal records documenting gestational age, birth weight, oxygen therapy, blood transfusions, and other ROP risk factors. • Documentation of counselling provided to parents regarding ROP risk and the importance of screening. • Written discharge summary with follow-up schedule and ophthalmology referral. • Referral records and appointment details for retinal screening. • Follow-up notes, including parental compliance and reminders where applicable. • Documentation of all communications, advice, and informed discussions with the family.

Effective communication and timely adherence to established screening protocols are as essential as clinical treatment in preventing avoidable lifelong disability.

30. Cetty Koteswara Rao

Full Case Name	Cetty Koteswara Rao v. M/s Apollo Hospitals
Citation / Case Number	First Appeal No. NC/FA/534/2023 (NCDRC)
Court / Forum	National Consumer Disputes Redressal Commission
Date of Judgment	5 February 2026
State / Jurisdiction	Andhra Pradesh
Type of Case	Consumer Protection / Medical Negligence / Burden of Proof

Background & Facts

Cetty Vijaya, the wife of the appellant Cetty Koteswara Rao, was suffering from Chronic Kidney Disease (CKD) Stage 5 - the most advanced stage of renal failure. For several years prior to this incident, she had been undergoing treatment at Seven Hills Hospital, Visakhapatnam, where she was advised to undergo hemodialysis three times per week. Despite medical treatment, her serum creatinine levels remained elevated. Out of frustration with slow progress, she began supplementing her treatment with herbal medicines for approximately 1.5 years - a decision made without professional guidance.

During this period of herbal self-treatment, she had **stopped hemodialysis entirely for 1.5 years**. By the time the couple sought a second opinion from Apollo Hospitals in July 2012, the patient was in a **critically deteriorated condition**. She presented with:

- Severe dyspnoea (shortness of breath) even at rest
- Orthopnoea (inability to breathe while lying down)
- Chest discomfort

- Fever with chills and rigours
- Pedal edema (swelling of feet)
- Past medical history of hypertension (previously operated) and hypothyroidism
- Highly irregular dialysis pattern

Upon admission to Apollo on 19 July 2012, the patient was immediately shifted to the Medical Intensive Care Unit (MICU). Clinical investigations revealed:

- Hemoglobin: 5.8 gm/dl (severe anemia)
- Total Leukocyte Count: 13,200 cells (elevated, indicating infection/sepsis)
- ESR: 65 mm/hr (very elevated, indicating severe inflammation)
- Urea: 195 mg/dl (severely elevated)
- Serum Creatinine: 106 mg/dl (severely elevated)
- Diagnosis: Acute kidney disease with hypervolemia (fluid overload) and sepsis

The hospital-initiated treatment with parenteral antibiotics, hemodialysis, and packed cell transfusion. The patient was placed on nebulization, antihypertensive medications, and oxygen therapy.

The patient was discharged on 20 August 2012 (32 days after admission). The hospital stated the discharge was **"against medical advice"** - meaning the doctors recommended continued hospitalization, but the family insisted on discharge. The family cited financial hardship (they had a bounced cheque for ₹ 1,00,000 and outstanding dues of ₹ 3 lakh). No discharge summary was collected by the family at the time of discharge (though one was prepared and available).

After discharge, the patient's condition deteriorated rapidly. She was moved to an Old Age Home and subsequently to Aditya Critical Care Centre, where she was declared **brain dead on 26 August 2012** - just 6 days after discharge from Apollo.

The appellant filed a consumer complaint alleging:

- Gross medical negligence in the treatment
- Deficiency in service (failure to provide discharge summary)
- Inappropriate care (patient placed in shared AC ward with other complicated patients, which affected her recovery)
- Improper discharge without oxygen support
- Failure to provide case sheet despite multiple RTI applications

Issues Raised

- Whether the hospital's treatment of a CKD Stage 5 patient in a critical condition with sepsis and multiple comorbidities constituted medical negligence.
- Whether the failure to provide a discharge summary at the time of discharge is a deficiency in service.
- Whether adverse clinical outcomes in critically ill patients automatically prove negligence.
- What burden of proof applies in medical negligence cases in consumer forums - is affidavit evidence and allegations sufficient, or is expert medical opinion mandatory?
- Whether a hospital can be held liable for a patient's death when the patient was already in terminal-stage disease before admission?

Arguments - Complainant / Appellant

- The treatment at Apollo resulted in complications: high blood pressure, body vibrations, unconsciousness - symptoms that were absent or controlled before admission.
- The patient's condition became critical on 28 July 2012 due to negligence by Apollo's doctors.
- The hospital discharged the patient against the family's wishes, in an emergency condition, without oxygen support in the ambulance.

- The patient was kept on ventilation from 28 July to 20 August (24 days) without adequate medical support or dialysis during hospitalization.
- The hospital failed to provide the case sheet and discharge summary, hindering the family's ability to obtain a second opinion or pursue legal remedies.
- The patient's placement in a shared AC ward with other critically ill patients compromised her care and contributed to her death.

Arguments - Respondent

- The patient was admitted in an already critical condition with CKD Stage 5, severe anaemia, active sepsis, hypervolemia, and multiple comorbidities.
- The patient had worsened her condition by abandoning haemodialysis for 1.5 years and resorting to unproven herbal treatment.
- The hospital provided standard, evidence-based care: antibiotics for sepsis, haemodialysis for uraemia, packed cell transfusion for severe anaemia, oxygen and antihypertensive drugs for respiratory and cardiovascular complications.
- The patient's clinical condition on discharge was **stable and improving** - this is documented in the case sheet.
- The discharge was **against the hospital's medical advice** - the doctors recommended continued hospitalization, but the family demanded discharge due to financial inability to pay.
- The discharge summary was prepared and ready; the family chose not to collect it.
- The patient's subsequent deterioration and death were due to her underlying advanced kidney disease, not hospital negligence.

- There is no expert evidence to prove that the hospital's treatment deviated from standard protocols or caused the patient's death.
- The family's financial stress should not be converted into a negligence claim against the hospital.

Judgment & Ruling

The NCDRC held that private hospitals can be held liable for deficiency in service under consumer law when there is proven medical negligence or failure to provide the expected standard of care. The commission examined whether the hospital and its medical staff had acted in accordance with reasonable medical practice in treating the patient. It reiterated that a hospital is responsible for the acts and omissions of its doctors and supporting staff under the principle of vicarious liability. The judgment clarified that mere dissatisfaction with treatment outcomes does not amount to negligence unless a breach of duty is established. It also emphasised the importance of expert evidence in assessing complex medical issues. This case reinforced accountability of private hospitals in India under the Consumer Protection framework. Both the State Consumer Disputes Redressal Commission (in the original complaint) and the National Consumer Disputes Redressal Commission (on appeal) dismissed the complaint and absolved Apollo Hospitals of liability.

Key Holdings:

- **Vague Allegations Without Expert Evidence Are Insufficient:**
  The appellant made allegations of negligcncc but could not point out any specific incident of negligence. Bald allegations without medical documents, expert evidence, or substantiated details cannot establish negligence.
- **Burden of Proof on Complainant:**

In medical negligence cases, the burden lies on the person alleging negligence to discharge this burden by presenting cogent evidence. Expert medical opinion is mandatory - affidavit alone is insufficient. The complainant's own application for permission to obtain expert opinion was dismissed by the State Commission itself.

- **Adverse Outcome ≠ Negligence:**
  The mere fact that a patient died does not establish medical negligence. "Deterioration of the condition of the patient post-surgery is not necessarily indicative... that the treatment given... was not proper... In some rare cases complications... arise but that by itself does not establish actionable negligence."
- **Standard of Care - Bolam Rule Applied:**
  The hospital exercised the skill of an ordinary competent medical professional. There was no apparent omission or breach of ethical protocol. The hospital followed acceptable medical practice and provided appropriate care to a critically ill patient.
- **Pre-Existing Terminal Illness is Context:**
  A patient admitted with CKD Stage 5 (end-stage renal disease requiring lifelong dialysis, with high mortality risk) cannot claim negligence merely because she died. The hospital did not cause the CKD; it attempted to manage an already critical condition.
- **Discharge Against Medical Advice is Not Negligence:**
  When a patient or family insists on discharge against the doctor's recommendation, and the patient was clinically stable or improving at the time of discharge, the hospital cannot be held liable for subsequent deterioration.
- **Financial Hardship is Not a Ground for Negligence:**
  The family's inability to pay bills cannot be converted into a claim of medical negligence. The hospital was entitled to insist on payment; the family's financial stress does not create a cause of action for negligence.

- **Lack of Discharge Summary Availability Is Not Proven:**
  The hospital stated it had prepared the discharge summary and it was available at the time of discharge. The family did not collect it. This is not a deficiency in service on the hospital's part.

Compensation / Outcome

The Supreme Court held that the complainant failed to establish medical negligence against Apollo Hospitals and the treating doctors. It observed that the patient's death, by itself, could not be treated as proof of negligence and that the medical professionals had acted in accordance with accepted medical practice. The Court set aside the compensation awarded by the consumer fora and dismissed the claim, reaffirming that liability cannot arise without proof of a breach of the required standard of care.

Significance & Impact:

Cetty Koteswara Rao v. M/s Apollo Hospitals reinforced the principle that doctors and hospitals are not insurers of successful medical outcomes. The judgment emphasised that courts must distinguish between an adverse result and actionable negligence, and that medical professionals should be judged by the standards of a reasonably competent practitioner. The decision strengthened the requirement of credible evidence in medical negligence claims and protected healthcare providers from liability based solely on unsuccessful treatment.

KEY LEGAL PRINCIPLES / RATIO DECIDENDI

- This case is a critical restatement of the evidentiary threshold for proving medical negligence in India's consumer forums.
- The judgment reinforces that mere allegations are insufficient; the complainant must present expert medical evidence to establish a breach of the standard of care.
- The commission emphasised the application of the Bolam Rule: a doctor is not negligent if he acts in accordance with acceptable norms of practice, and a mere deviation or adverse outcome does not prove negligence without expert evidence to the contrary.
- The judgment also clarifies that consumer forums cannot be used as a substitute for proper medical evidence - they cannot infer negligence from vague allegations or the fact that a patient died.
- A hospital treating a terminally ill patient (CKD Stage 5) is not liable for the patient's death unless it is proven that the treatment fell below the standard of reasonable competence.
- The decision protects hospitals from frivolous claims where grieving families, frustrated by poor outcomes in end-stage disease, allege negligence without substantiation.
- However, it also serves as a cautionary reminder that without expert evidence, no medical negligence case can succeed - burden is entirely on the complainant.
- This case is often cited to emphasize that procedure must accompany passion in medical negligence litigation.

MEDLEX360 PRACTICE PEARLS	
What went wrong?	No medical negligence was established because the allegations were unsupported by specific evidence or expert opinion, while the hospital's records showed appropriate treatment and discharge against medical advice (DAMA).
Risk Management Takeaways	• Follow accepted clinical protocols and document adherence. • Clearly document DAMA discussions, risks explained, and patient/family decision. • Maintain complete, contemporaneous medical records. • Prepare and provide (or document availability of) the discharge summary. • Record the patient's clinical status at admission and discharge. • Ensure all communication with the patient/family is documented.
Documentation Checklist	• Admission assessment, diagnosis, and comorbidities. • Investigation reports and treatment records. • Daily progress notes and specialist reviews. • Dialysis, transfusion, and critical care documentation. • DAMA form with risks explained and signatures. • Discharge summary with documented handover/collection. • Records of counselling and discussions with the family.

Good documentation is the strongest defence when appropriate medical care is questioned.

31. Poonam Verma (Cross-Pathy: Negligence Per Se)

Full Case Name	Poonam Verma v. Dr. Ashwin Patel & Ors.
Citation / Case Number	(1996) 4 SCC 332; 1996 AIR 2111
Court / Forum	Supreme Court of India
Date of Judgment	10 May 1996
State / Jurisdiction	Maharashtra (Bombay)
Type of Case	Negligence Per Se / Consumer Protection

Background & Facts

Pramod Verma, a 35-year-old salaried employee, developed fever on 4 July 1992. He consulted Dr. Ashwin Patel, who was a registered practitioner of Homoeopathic Medicine and Surgery (DHMS - Diploma in Homeopathic Medicine and Surgery, obtained from Homeopathic Medical College, Anand, Gujarat). Dr. Patel was registered with the Gujarat Homeopathic Medical Council under the Bombay Homoeopathic Practitioners Act, 1959.

Despite his qualification and registration **only in homoeopathy**, Dr. Patel prescribed **allopathic medicines** - strong antibiotics - to treat Pramod Verma's fever. He initially diagnosed viral fever and prescribed allopathic antibiotics until 6 July 1992. When the patient's condition did not improve, he changed the diagnosis to typhoid fever and continued prescribing allopathic antibiotics.

Critical breaches:

- **No diagnostic confirmation:**
  Dr. Patel did not order blood tests or urine examinations to confirm either viral fever or typhoid.
- **Oral advice instead of written:**
  When asked about pathological tests, Dr. Patel claimed he had advised them orally, but medical practice requires written prescriptions for pathological investigations. This was contrary to usual medical conduct.
- **Prescribing outside qualified system:**
  Dr. Patel was treating the patient with allopathic medicines while being registered and qualified only in homoeopathy.

Pramod Verma's condition deteriorated rapidly under this treatment. On 12 July 1992, he was shifted to Sanjeevani Maternity and General Nursing Home under Dr. Rajeev Warty (Respondent No. 2) on Dr. Patel's advice. He remained there until 14 July 1992, when he was transferred to Hinduja Hospital in an **unconscious state**. He died approximately 4.5 hours after admission to Hinduja Hospital.

Poonam Verma, the widow, filed a complaint before the National Consumer Disputes Redressal Commission (NCDRC) alleging negligence and deficiency in service. The NCDRC initially dismissed her petition. However, on appeal, the Supreme Court overturned the decision and held Dr. Patel liable for medical negligence.

Issues Raised

- Whether a doctor registered to practice one system of medicine (homoeopathy) can legally and without negligence prescribe medicines of another system (allopathy) for which he is not qualified or registered.
- Whether the practice of a non-qualified system of medicine without formal registration constitutes negligence per se (negligence by itself, without requiring further proof of breach of standard of care).

- Whether the failure to order diagnostic tests (blood/urine) before prescribing treatment for fever constitutes medical negligence.
- Whether oral advice for pathological investigations can substitute for written prescriptions as per standard medical practice.
- Whether the patient's death, occurring under this treatment, was directly caused by the doctor's negligence.?

Arguments - Complainant / Appellant

- Dr. Ashwin Patel was registered only with the Gujarat Homeopathic Medical Council and had no registration or formal qualifications in allopathic medicine.
- Prescribing allopathic medicines - especially strong antibiotics - without proper qualification and without confirming diagnosis through investigations, constitutes medical negligence.
- The doctor did not order blood tests or urine examination before or during treatment, relying instead on clinical guess.
- The usual practice of doctors is to provide written prescriptions for pathological investigations; oral advice is insufficient and contrary to medical norms.
- The patient's condition deteriorated under the doctor's treatment, suggesting the diagnosis and/or treatment were incorrect.
- The patient died shortly after being transferred to another hospital, raising questions about the adequacy of prior treatment.

Arguments - Respondent

- He had undertaken an integrated course of study covering subjects such as Anatomy, Physiology, Pathology, Forensic Medicine, Surgery, Practice of Medicine, Hygiene, Midwifery, and Gynaecology as part of his DHMS curriculum.

- Therefore, he had theoretical knowledge of allopathic medicine and was competent to prescribe allopathic medicines.
- He exercised reasonable clinical judgment in diagnosing viral fever initially and then typhoid fever based on symptoms common in the locality.
- He had advised the patient to undergo pathological tests (orally), but the patient did not comply.
- The patient's deterioration and death were due to the severity of the illness, not due to negligence in treatment.
- Many homoeopathic doctors in practice also prescribe allopathic medicines as complementary treatment.

Judgment & Ruling

The Supreme Court of India held that a person who does not possess the requisite medical qualification but still practices medicine is liable for negligence per se. The Court distinguished between negligence by a qualified doctor and treatment by an unqualified practitioner, holding the latter as inherently unlawful. In this case, a homeopathic doctor prescribed allopathic medicines, which resulted in the patient's death. The Court ruled that such conduct amounted to gross negligence and could not be justified under any circumstances. It emphasised that patients have a right to receive treatment only from properly qualified medical professionals. The judgment strengthened consumer protection and accountability in medical practice in India. The Court awarded ₹3 lakhs compensation to Poonam Verma, plus ₹30,000 as costs.

Key Holdings:

- **Practicing a Non-Qualified System Is Negligence Per Se:**
  A medical practitioner who practices a system of medicine for which he is not formally qualified, registered, or licensed commits negligence per se. Negligence per se means that the

very act of practicing outside one's registered qualifications is inherently negligent - no further proof of breach of standard of care is required.

- **Theoretical Knowledge ≠ Professional Qualification:**
  Having covered certain subjects (like Anatomy) in a homoeopathy curriculum does not qualify a doctor to practice allopathic medicine. Professional medical systems are distinct; each has its own pharmacology, dosages, contraindications, and treatment protocols. A doctor must be formally educated, trained, and registered in a system before practicing it.
- **Registration Defines Scope of Practice:**
  The Bombay Homoeopathic Practitioners Act, 1959 and the Homoeopathy Central Council Act, 1973 clearly delineate that practitioners registered under these Acts are authorized to practice homoeopathy only. Practice of allopathy by a homoeopath is a violation of statute and of medical ethics.
- **Diagnostic Tests Are Mandatory Before Prescribing Treatment:**
  Before prescribing antibiotics or other systemic medicines for fever, a doctor must order confirmatory investigations (blood culture, blood tests, urine examination) to establish the diagnosis. Prescribing strong antibiotics based solely on clinical suspicion and symptoms (which could fit multiple diagnoses) is negligent.
- **Written Prescriptions Are Standard Practice:**
  When a doctor advises pathological tests, the usual and expected practice is to write these on a prescription. Oral advice to undergo tests, followed by the patient not complying, suggests either the advice was not given clearly or the doctor did not consider it important enough to formalize. The Court rejected the doctor's claim of oral advice as contrary to standard medical practice.
- **The Bolam Rule Applied Within Scope of Qualifications:**

While doctors are not expected to use the highest degree of skill and some latitude is given for clinical judgment, this protection applies only within the doctor's field of qualification and registration. A doctor practicing outside his registered field has no such protection.

- **Violation of Statutory Duty = Actionable Negligence:**
  The practice of allopathic medicine by a registered homoeopath violates the statutory framework governing medical practice in India. This statutory violation automatically constitutes negligence and gives rise to a cause of action for compensation.

Compensation / Outcome

The Supreme Court held Dr. Ashwin Patel liable for medical negligence for treating a patient beyond his area of competence. The doctor, who was registered as a homeopathic practitioner, prescribed allopathic medicines to the patient, which was beyond the scope of his permitted practice. The Court held that this amounted to negligence *per se* and awarded compensation to the patient's legal representatives for the resulting harm.

Significance & Impact:

Poonam Verma v. Dr. Ashwin Patel & Ors. is a landmark judgment establishing that practicing a branch of medicine without the requisite qualification or authorization constitutes medical negligence. The Court distinguished between an error of judgment by a qualified doctor and treatment by a person lacking the necessary expertise, holding the latter to be a clear breach of professional duty. The decision strengthened standards of medical licensing, professional competence, and patient protection in healthcare law.

KEY LEGAL PRINCIPLES / RATIO DECIDENDI

- This is a landmark judgment establishing the doctrine of "negligence per se" in the context of Indian medical practice.
- The Supreme Court clarified that India's medical regulatory framework recognizes distinct systems of medicine (Allopathy, Homoeopathy, Ayurveda, Unani, etc.), and each has separate registration and licensing requirements.
- A practitioner registered in one system cannot legally or without negligence practice another system, even if they have theoretical knowledge of its subjects.
- This judgment has profound implications in India where:
    a) Integrated DHMS courses teach comparative anatomy and pathology, but this theoretical
    b) knowledge does not authorize practice in allopathy;
    c) Many unqualified practitioners falsely claim integrated training;
    d) Patients often do not know whether their doctor is allopathic, homoeopathic, or ayurvedic.
- The Court held that practicing outside one's registered system is negligence per se - meaning the violation is self-evident and requires no expert evidence to establish it as a breach. This differs from clinical negligence (deviating from standard treatment protocols), which usually requires expert testimony.
- The judgment reinforces the importance of proper diagnostic investigation before prescribing systemic medicines and establishes that oral advice for investigations does not meet the standard expected of competent practitioners.
- This case is foundational for understanding the regulatory boundaries between India's medical systems and has been cited extensively to discipline doctors practicing outside their qualified domain.

MEDLEX360 PRACTICE PEARLS	
What went wrong?	A homoeopathic practitioner treated a patient with allopathic medicines without being qualified to do so and without adequate diagnostic evaluation or proper documentation, amounting to negligence per se.
Risk Management Takeaways	• Practice only within your registered system of medicine. • Confirm the diagnosis with appropriate investigations before initiating treatment. • Document all advised investigations and treatment plans in writing. • Do not rely on oral instructions for essential investigations. • Refer the patient promptly when the required expertise is beyond your scope of practice. • Ensure prescriptions comply with statutory and professional requirements.
Documentation Checklist	• Diagnosis and differential diagnosis. • Written prescriptions for medicines and investigations. • Relevant laboratory reports before initiating treatment, where indicated. • Patient consent and counselling regarding diagnosis and treatment. • Referral notes, if the patient's condition requires specialist care. • Complete clinical records with dated progress notes.

A doctor's competence is defined by their qualification and registration - practising beyond that boundary invites both patient harm and legal liability.

32. Paschim Banga Khet Mazdoor Samiti

Full Case Name	Paschim Banga Khet Mazdoor Samiti & Ors. v. State of West Bengal & Anr.
Citation / Case Number	(1996) 4 SCC 37; 1996 AIR SC 2426; JT 1996 (6) 43
Court / Forum	Supreme Court of India
Date of Judgment	06 May 1996
State / Jurisdiction	West Bengal
Type of Case	Constitutional Law / Public Interest Litigation / Right to Emergency Medical Care under Article 21

Background & Facts

Hakim Sheikh, an agricultural labourer and member of the Paschim Banga Khet Mazdoor Samiti (West Bengal Agricultural Labour Union), accidentally fell off a running train at Mathurapur Station, West Bengal, at approximately 7:45 PM on 8 July 1992. The fall caused severe head injuries and brain haemorrhage - a life-threatening emergency requiring immediate neurosurgical intervention.

What followed was a harrowing 14-hour ordeal across eight government hospitals in and around Calcutta, during which Hakim Sheikh was refused admission at every State-run facility he was taken to:

- **Primary Health Centre, Mathurapur:**
  Provided first aid but lacked facilities for neurosurgical treatment. Referred him to Diamond Harbour Sub-Divisional Hospital or any available State hospital.

- **Neel Ratan Sircar (N.R.S.) Medical College Hospital, Calcutta (11:45 PM, 8 July 1992):** Emergency Medical Officer examined him, took two skull X-rays, and recommended immediate admission. However, could not be admitted in the Surgery Department (which had neurosurgery facilities) as there was no vacant bed in the Surgical Emergency Ward or the regular surgery ward.
- **Calcutta Medical College Hospital:** Refused admission due to non-availability of beds.
- **Calcutta National Medical College Hospital:** Refused admission due to non-availability of beds.
- **Bangur Institute of Neurology (early morning, 9 July 1992)** Refused admission due to non-availability of beds.
- **Further hospitals approached:** All State hospitals with neurosurgery facilities reported full bed occupancy.

Finally, on 9 July 1992, Hakim Sheikh was admitted to Calcutta Medical Research Institute (CMRI) - a private hospital - where he received indoor treatment until 22 July 1992. He incurred a medical bill of approximately ₹17,000 - an enormous sum for an agricultural labourer - for treatment that should have been available to him free of cost at any government hospital.

Feeling aggrieved by what they described as the “indifferent and callous attitude” of the medical authorities at multiple State-run hospitals, the Paschim Banga Khet Mazdoor Samiti and Hakim Sheikh filed a writ petition before the Supreme Court under Article 32 of the Constitution, alleging that the State of West Bengal had violated Hakim Sheikh's fundamental right to life under Article 21 by failing to provide him timely emergency medical care.

During the pendency of the petition, the State Government appointed an Enquiry Committee headed by Justice Lilamoy Ghose, a retired Judge of the Calcutta High Court, to investigate the incident and recommend systemic remedies.

Issues Raised

- Whether the right to life under Article 21 of the Constitution includes the right to emergency medical care and treatment at State-run hospitals.
- Whether the failure of government hospitals to admit and treat a critically injured person - due to non-availability of beds or facilities - constitutes a violation of the fundamental right to life.
- Whether the State can escape constitutional responsibility by pleading lack of financial resources or infrastructural constraints as justification for denial of emergency care.
- Whether the Supreme Court, under Article 32, has the power to award monetary compensation for violation of fundamental rights.
- What systemic and structural reforms are required to prevent recurrence of such incidents across India?

Arguments - Petitioners

- Hakim Sheikh's right to life under Article 21 was violated when he was denied emergency medical treatment despite presenting to multiple government hospitals in a life-threatening condition.
- The State of West Bengal runs and maintains these hospitals with public funds and is constitutionally obligated to ensure that its citizens receive timely medical care, especially in emergencies.
- The 14-hour ordeal across eight hospitals - during which the patient had brain haemorrhage - could easily have cost him his life. The indifference shown by the hospitals is unconstitutional.
- Financial hardship and infrastructure constraints are no excuse for violating fundamental rights.
- The patient incurred ₹17,000 in costs at a private hospital for treatment that should have been provided free at a State facility; this expenditure must be compensated.

- The situation calls for systemic judicial intervention to create binding standards for emergency care at all government hospitals.

Arguments - Respondent

- The State runs 57,875 hospital beds across West Bengal, of which 90% are free beds for poor patients.
- All neurosurgery beds in government hospitals in Calcutta were genuinely occupied on the night of 8-9 July 1992; this was not indifference but a resource constraint.
- The State had already initiated an inquiry into the incident through the Lilamoy Ghose Committee and had taken corrective action.
- Financial resources are not unlimited; the State cannot be held constitutionally liable for the unavailability of beds in over-crowded hospitals.
- The medical officers provided first aid and X-rays and made efforts to find a hospital; they were not indifferent to the patient's condition.

Judgment & Ruling

The Supreme Court allowed the writ petition and held the State of West Bengal liable for violation of Hakim Sheikh's fundamental right under Article 21. The Court awarded ₹25,000 as compensation (of which ₹15,000 had already been paid as interim compensation during the proceedings; the balance of ₹10,000 was directed to be paid within one month). The Supreme Court held that the failure of government hospitals to provide timely emergency medical treatment amounts to a violation of the right to life under Article 21 of the Constitution. The Court observed that the State has a constitutional obligation to preserve human life and cannot deny treatment on grounds such as lack of beds, facilities, or resources. It ruled that in emergency situations, every government hospital must extend immediate medical aid and, if necessary, refer the patient to another suitable facility without delay. The judgment expanded the scope of the right to health as an integral part of the right to life. It directed the State to improve emergency medical infrastructure and ensure effective coordination among hospitals.

Key Holdings:

- **Right to Life Includes Right to Emergency Medical Care:**
  Article 21 of the Constitution imposes an obligation on the State to safeguard the right to life of every person. Preservation of human life is of paramount importance. Government hospitals run by the State and medical officers employed therein are duty-bound to extend medical assistance for preserving human life.
- **Denial of Emergency Care = Violation of Article 21:**
  Failure on the part of a government hospital to provide timely medical treatment to a person in need of such treatment results in violation of his right to life guaranteed under Article 21. This is the first Supreme Court judgment to expressly hold that denial of emergency medical treatment by a government hospital is a constitutional violation.
- **Financial Constraints Are No Defence:**
  The State cannot claim lack of financial resources as justification for denying citizens their fundamental rights guaranteed under Part III of the Constitution. The constitutional obligation to provide adequate medical services cannot be ignored on account of financial burden.
- **No Bed Cannot Mean No Care:**
  A patient in a critical, life-threatening condition cannot be turned away from a government hospital simply because no bed is available. The Emergency Medical Officer must contact superior authority by telephone if beds are not available and ensure the patient is admitted despite stringency. Alternatively, the hospital must ensure immediate transfer to a facility where care can be provided

- not simply refer the patient elsewhere and discharge all responsibility.

- **State Vicariously Responsible for Hospital Officers:** Since the denial of Hakim Sheikh's right was by officers of the State in hospitals run by the State, the State cannot avoid its constitutional responsibility. Individual medical officers responsible for the lapses were to be subject to departmental action.
- **Supreme Court Can Award Compensation for Fundamental Rights Violations:**
  Under Article 32, the Supreme Court has the power to award monetary compensation as a remedy for violation of fundamental rights - not just issue directions or declaratory orders.
- **Systemic Reforms Are Mandatory:**
  The Court issued comprehensive systemic directions (adopting the Lilamoy Ghose Committee's recommendations), binding on all States, including:
    - Primary Health Centres must provide first aid and stabilize patients before referral;
    - Emergency Medical Officers must admit critically ill patients in consultation with specialist duty doctors regardless of bed availability, coordinating with superiors to create space
    - No patient in a life-threatening condition can be refused admission solely on grounds of non-availability of beds
    - All States must upgrade emergency healthcare infrastructure to meet the growing needs of the population
    - A centralized ambulance service with all necessary life-support equipment must be created
    - Emergency units at hospitals must be fully equipped and a medical officer must be available round the clock.

Compensation / Outcome

The Supreme Court held the State of West Bengal responsible for failing to provide timely emergency medical treatment to a person who suffered serious injuries after being denied admission by several government hospitals. The Court awarded ₹25,000 as compensation to the injured person and directed the State to improve its healthcare infrastructure, including ensuring the availability of emergency facilities and timely medical assistance in government hospitals.

Significance & Impact:

Paschim Banga Khet Mazdoor Samiti & Ors. v. State of West Bengal & Anr. is a landmark judgment recognizing the right to emergency medical care as a fundamental right under Article 21 of the Constitution. The Court held that the State has a constitutional obligation to maintain adequate medical facilities and cannot avoid responsibility due to lack of resources or infrastructure. The decision strengthened patients' rights, imposed affirmative duties on governments to provide accessible healthcare, and became a foundational precedent in the development of public health jurisprudence in India.

KEY LEGAL PRINCIPLES / RATIO DECIDENDI

- This is one of India's most consequential judgments on the constitutional dimensions of healthcare.
- Building on Parmanand Katara (1989 - no medico-legal formalities before emergency treatment), the Supreme Court in Paschim Banga took the jurisprudence decisively further: it held that the right to emergency medical care is not merely a professional obligation of doctors or a policy aspiration of the State - it is a **fundamental**

constitutional right of every Indian citizen enforceable under Article 21.

- The State's failure to provide timely emergency care is not an administrative lapse; it is a **constitutional violation** for which the State is liable to pay compensation.
- The judgment is path-breaking on three fronts:
  a) It extended the content of Article 21 to include the right to health and emergency medical care;
  b) It held that financial constraints and infrastructural limitations cannot justify denial of fundamental rights; and
  c) It issued binding pan-India systemic directions for emergency healthcare reform.
- This case is cited globally as an example of judicial enforcement of socio-economic rights through constitutional interpretation.
- It is the foundational authority for all subsequent litigation on denial of emergency medical care in Indian courts and consumer forums, and has been referenced in landmark judgments from South Africa and other common law countries examining the justiciability of the right to health.

MEDLEX360 PRACTICE PEARLS	
What went wrong?	A critically injured patient was denied timely emergency treatment by multiple government hospitals due to bed unavailability, resulting in a violation of his constitutional right to life under Article 21.
Risk Management Takeaways	• Never refuse emergency care solely due to non-availability of beds. • Stabilize every emergency patient before referral. • Escalate bed shortages immediately to senior authorities.

MEDLEX360 PRACTICE PEARLS	
	• Ensure coordinated transfer to an appropriate facility with prior communication. • Maintain functional emergency and ambulance services round the clock. • Follow established emergency triage and referral protocols. • Recognize that resource constraints do not excuse denial of emergency care.
Documentation Checklist	• Time of arrival and triage assessment. • Clinical findings and emergency stabilization provided. • Reason for referral or transfer. • Bed availability status and escalation efforts. • Communication with receiving hospital and senior authorities. • Transfer arrangements and ambulance details. • Patient/attendant counselling and informed communication.

In a medical emergency, no patient should be denied life-saving care because of administrative or resource constraints.

33. Arun Kumar Manglik

Full Case Name	Arun Kumar Manglik v. Chirayu Health and Medicare Private Ltd. & Anr.
Citation / Case Number	(2019) 7 SCC 401; Civil Appeal Nos. 227-228 of 2019 (@SLP(C) Nos. 30119-30120 of 2016)
Court / Forum	Supreme Court of India
Date of Judgment	9 January 2019
State / Jurisdiction	Madhya Pradesh
Type of Case	Consumer Protection / Medical Negligence / Standard of Care / Monitoring Protocols

Background & Facts

Madhu Manglik, aged 56 years, was diagnosed with dengue fever on 14 November 2009. A pathological laboratory report from Glaze Pathology that day showed: RBC 4.21 million/cmm, Haemoglobin 12.1 gm/dL, TLC 1,900/cmm, Platelet Count 1,79,000/cmm, and Dengue NS1 Antigen Positive. Critically, her platelet count had already begun declining - a recognised warning sign in dengue progression. She had a significant past medical history including catheter ablation and paroxysmal supraventricular tachycardia (PSVT), indicating pre-existing cardiac vulnerability. She had also been on an aspirin regimen for her cardiac condition prior to admission - a fact disclosed to the treating doctors at the time of admission.

On the advice of Dr. Ajay Goenka (Respondent No. 2, Director of the hospital), she was admitted to Chirayu Health and Medicare Private Ltd., Bhopal at approximately 7:00 AM on 15 November 2009 and immediately placed in the Intensive Care Unit (ICU). Although afebrile at the time of admission, she presented with headache, body ache, and a general sense of restlessness - classic accompanying signs of dengue fever.

Blood investigations at 7:30 AM on admission showed a precipitous decline in platelet count from 1,79,000 (previous day) to 97,000/cumm, Haemoglobin 13.4 gm/dL, TLC 3,000/cumm, SGPT elevated at 521 U/L, SGOT at 105 mg/dL - a sharp overnight deterioration signalling that the patient was transitioning toward dengue's critical phase. At 10:00 AM her pulse was 88/min, BP 130/88 mmHg, and she was afebrile.

The critical failure: Despite these warning signs of rapid progression, no further blood monitoring was conducted throughout the day. The hospital administered approximately 1,200 ml of intravenous fluids between 7:00 AM and 6:00 PM. Neither haematocrit (HCT) levels nor platelet counts were re-checked during this critical 11-hour window.

At 6:00 PM, the patient developed bradycardia (abnormally slow heart rate) and the fluid infusion was increased by 1.5 litres. Only at 7:15 PM - after she had already developed signs of acute cardiac distress - were blood investigations repeated. Results showed a catastrophic deterioration: Haemoglobin had crashed to 8.1 gm/dL, Platelet Count had fallen to just 19,000/cmm, Total protein 3.9 gm%, SGOT 169 IU/L. At 8:00 PM, the patient suffered cardiac arrest. She was declared dead at 8:50 PM.

Key additional facts:

- Dr. Ajay Goenka, the hospital's director and the treating doctor who had advised admission, was on leave and out of station the entire day on 15 November 2009. He never personally visited the patient.
- He consulted telephonically with a senior doctor, Dr. N.P. Mishra, but this consultation was remote and unsupported by direct clinical examination.
- The treating resident, Dr. Abhay Tyagi, was the primary doctor on the ground.

The Medical Council of India's Ethics Committee, after investigation on 20 February 2015, concluded that while the treatment protocol was correct as per medical guidelines, it was **not administered timely**. The Ethics Committee found prima facie professional misconduct by both Dr. Ajay Goenka and Dr. Abhay Tyagi and issued both a formal warning, directing them to be more careful in future.

Arun Kumar Manglik, the deceased's husband, filed a complaint before the MP State Consumer Disputes Redressal Commission (SCDRC) seeking ₹48 lakhs compensation. The SCDRC found medical negligence established and awarded ₹6 lakhs with 9% interest per annum. The NCDRC reversed this finding entirely. The Supreme Court, on appeal, restored the finding of negligence and enhanced the compensation.

Issues Raised

- Whether the failure to conduct regular haematological monitoring (platelet count, HCT levels) in a confirmed dengue patient in the ICU constitutes medical negligence.
- Whether the WHO guidelines on dengue management and the Directorate of National Vector Borne Disease Control Programme (NVBDCP) 2008 protocols form part of the standard of care in India.
- Whether the treating doctor's failure to physically attend a critically ill patient admitted on his advice constitutes professional misconduct and negligence.
- Whether the NCDRC was justified in reversing the SCDRC's well-reasoned finding of negligence.
- How compensation should be calculated for the death of a non-employed spouse.
- Whether the Bolam test requires reconsideration in light of Article 21 and the Bolitho refinement.

Arguments - Complainant / Appellant

- The WHO dengue guidelines (Clause 2.3.2.2) and NVBDCP 2008 protocols (Clause 7.1) explicitly mandate close monitoring of platelet counts, haematocrit, temperature, fluid balance, and vital signs during the critical phase. These guidelines were not followed.
- The platelet count had shown a steep decline even before admission - from 1,79,000 to 97,000 in less than 24 hours. This trajectory unmistakably signalled approaching dengue shock syndrome. The hospital had all the information needed to anticipate the crisis and act.
- No haematocrit monitoring was conducted between 7:30 AM and 7:15 PM - an 11-hour gap in a patient who was deteriorating in real time. This gap is inexcusable and directly caused the fatal delay in intervention.
- Fluid administration of approximately 1,200 ml without concurrent blood level monitoring directly contributed to the patient's deterioration; plasma leakage and haemodilution went undetected until it was too late.
- Dr. Goenka, who had personally advised the patient's admission to his hospital, abandoned his professional responsibility by remaining out of station on the very day his critically ill patient was admitted and never physically examining her.
- The NCDRC's finding that the family's administration of aspirin was a contributing cause was unjustified: the aspirin history was fully disclosed to the treating team at admission, documented in medical records, and was therefore a known variable that should have informed the treatment plan.
- The NCDRC reversed a well-reasoned SCDRC judgment without adequate basis or justification.

Arguments - Respondent

- The patient was admitted in a stable condition on 15 November 2009 with a platelet count of 97,000/cumm - not yet at the threshold for platelet transfusion (which per WHO and MP Government guidelines is required only when platelets fall below 20,000/cumm in the absence of haemorrhagic tendency).
- The treatment protocol followed - IV fluids, monitoring, investigation - was consistent with accepted medical guidelines.
- The patient was attended by a team of four qualified doctors, including Dr. Abhay Tyagi (MBBS with ICU experience) and Dr. Atul Singhal; she was not left unattended.
- Dr. Goenka was on leave but remained available telephonically and consulted with Dr. N.P. Mishra regarding the patient.
- The aspirin administered by the patient's family before admission - without informing the hospital - could have independently contributed to the patient's haemorrhagic complications.
- The patient's death was an outcome of dengue shock syndrome, a disease that can deteriorate rapidly despite appropriate care.
- Dengue shock syndrome is a known, serious complication of dengue fever with inherent unpredictability; its occurrence is not evidence of negligence.

Judgment & Ruling

The Supreme Court held the hospital liable for medical negligence in the treatment of a dengue patient who died due to inadequate monitoring and delayed medical intervention. The Court found that the hospital failed to adhere to the standard treatment protocols and WHO guidelines by not timely monitoring critical blood parameters, thereby falling below the standard of reasonable care expected under the *Bolam* test. The Court restored the finding of negligence against the hospital, set aside the National Consumer Disputes Redressal Commission's order exonerating it, enhanced the compensation from ₹6 lakh to ₹15 lakh with interest, and clarified that the hospital's Director was not personally liable as he was not the treating doctor.

Key Holdings:

- **Failure to monitor in real-time is negligence:** Except for the blood sample which was taken at about 7:30 AM, no further effort was made to determine haematocrit levels during the course of the day, and it was only when the patient suffered a cardiac arrest after 6:00 PM that blood investigations were done at about 7:15 PM. This absence of monitoring during a critical 11-hour window, in a patient already showing a precipitous platelet decline, was found to be direct medical negligence. The doctors precluded themselves from receiving critical information about the disease's progression.
- **WHO and NVBDCP guidelines define the standard of care:** The WHO dengue guidelines and the NVBDCP 2008 protocols are not aspirational documents - they define the minimum standard of care expected when treating dengue in India. Adherence to these guidelines is mandatory for hospitals treating confirmed dengue cases. Deviation from them is prima facie evidence of negligence.
- **Patient-centric approach is mandatory:** While treating a patient, medical professionals should adopt a patient-centric approach. The treating team's failure to dynamically adjust monitoring and management based on the patient's evolving clinical condition - particularly given her cardiac history and rapidly declining platelets - was inconsistent with this standard.
- **The attending doctor cannot remain absent:** Dr. Goenka admitted the patient on his advice and assurance. His failure to physically attend the patient on the day of

admission - choosing to remain out of station and consult only by telephone - constituted professional misconduct. The Ethics Committee of the MCI independently confirmed this finding.

- **Aspirin history was known and must be factored into treatment:** The fact that the patient had taken aspirin was disclosed to the treating team at the time of admission and was documented in medical records. The NCDRC was wrong to attribute fault to the family for prior aspirin use. Once the treating doctors were aware of this factor, it became their responsibility to adjust the management plan accordingly - to monitor more vigilantly for haemorrhagic complications.

  Bolitho refinement of Bolam applied: While the Bolam test continues to govern the standard of care, the Court applied the Bolitho refinement: a body of professional opinion that is not capable of withstanding logical analysis cannot provide a defence. The hospital's claim that its treatment was within acceptable practice could not survive scrutiny when the monitoring protocol it followed was directly contrary to published WHO and NVBDCP guidelines.
- **Compensation for non-employed spouse:** The loss of a non-employed spouse is compensable and must account for household contribution, companionship, and future dependency. The Court applied the principles from National Insurance Company Ltd. v. Pranay Sethi, with suitable modifications, to arrive at enhanced compensation of ₹15 lakhs.

Compensation / Outcome

The Supreme Court upheld the finding of medical negligence against Chirayu Health and Medicare Private Ltd. and the treating doctors, holding the hospital liable for failure to provide proper post-operative care and monitoring after surgery. The Court affirmed the compensation awarded to the complainant, recognizing that the patient's death resulted from deficiencies in treatment and management rather than an unavoidable medical complication. It emphasised that hospitals owe a duty of care not only during procedures but also during post-operative recovery and supervision.

Significance & Impact:

Arun Kumar Manglik v. Chirayu Health and Medicare Private Ltd. & Anr. is an important judgment on hospital accountability and deficiency in medical services. The Supreme Court reiterated that healthcare institutions can be held liable for failures in systems of care, including inadequate monitoring and management of patients after treatment. The decision expanded the understanding of medical negligence beyond individual acts of doctors and highlighted the institutional responsibility of hospitals to maintain appropriate standards of patient care.

KEY LEGAL PRINCIPLES / RATIO DECIDENDI

- This case is a landmark in three distinct but interconnected areas of Indian medical negligence law. First, it establishes that published clinical guidelines (WHO, NVBDCP, national health ministry protocols) are not merely advisory - they define the standard of care in consumer forums and courts. A hospital that fails to follow these guidelines cannot shelter behind the general Bolam defence. Second, the case introduced the concept of a "patient-centric approach" as an enforceable legal standard in India - a doctor cannot design treatment around institutional convenience, resource constraints, or professional availability; the patient's evolving condition must be the centre of every clinical decision. Third, it is the first Supreme Court judgment authored by Justice D.Y. Chandrachud (later CJI) on medical negligence, and it flagged that the Bolam test itself may require reconsideration in the context of Article 21 and the Bolitho reasonableness requirement - a signal that future courts may apply a higher, patient-rights-oriented standard. This case is essential reading for any clinician treating infectious diseases with dynamic progression (dengue, malaria, sepsis, enteric fever) and for any lawyer advising on failure-to-monitor claims.

MEDLEX360 PRACTICE PEARLS	
What went wrong?	The treating team failed to provide timely serial monitoring and reassessment of a high-risk dengue patient despite clear warning signs of rapid deterioration, resulting in delayed recognition and management of the patient's critical condition.
Risk Management Takeaways	• Monitor **trends**, not just isolated laboratory values. • Follow recognised clinical guidelines unless deviation is justified and documented. • Ensure timely consultant review or documented handover. • Escalate care promptly when warning signs appear. • Document all reassessments, decisions, and clinical reasoning.
Documentation Checklist	• Baseline history, comorbidities, medications, and risk assessment. • Initial and serial platelet count, haematocrit, and other relevant investigations.

MEDLEX360 PRACTICE PEARLS

- Vital signs, urine output, and fluid balance chart.
- Time-stamped consultant reviews and treatment modifications.
- Documentation of clinical deterioration and escalation.
- Family counselling and informed discussions.
- Handover and consultant availability records

In critical illness, timely monitoring is as important as timely treatment.

34. Dr. Jayshree Ujwal Ingole

Full Case Name	Dr. Sou Jayshree Ujwal Ingole v. State of Maharashtra & Anr.
Citation / Case Number	Criminal Appeal No. 636 of 2017 (Arising out of SLP (Crl.) No. 7186 of 2014); (2018) 1 SCC (Cri) 145; AIR 2017 SC 2078
Court / Forum	Supreme Court of India
Date of Judgment	6 April 2017
State / Jurisdiction	Pan-India
Type of Case	Criminal - Medical Negligence (Section 304-A IPC)

Background & Facts

The case arose from the death of a patient suffering from **haemophilia**, who was admitted to Irvin Hospital, Amravati, following injuries sustained in a road traffic accident. The patient remained under the care of several doctors, including **Dr. Sou Jayshree Ujwal Ingole**, and later died due to excessive bleeding and complications.

A criminal case under **Section 304-A IPC** was registered against multiple doctors alleging negligent medical treatment. One of the treating doctors had already been discharged from the proceedings, whereas criminal prosecution continued against Dr. Ingole. She approached the Bombay High Court seeking quashing of the criminal proceedings under Section 482 CrPC, but the High Court declined relief. She thereafter appealed to the Supreme Court.

Issues Raised

- Whether the allegations disclosed **criminal negligence** sufficient to prosecute a doctor under Section 304-A IPC.

- Whether an **error of clinical judgment** amounts to criminal negligence.
- Whether the evidence established **gross negligence** as required by law.
- Whether continuation of criminal proceedings amounted to abuse of the process of law.

Judgment & Ruling

The Supreme Court **allowed the appeal**, set aside the High Court's order, and **quashed the criminal proceedings** against Dr. Ingole. It held that her conduct, at most, was an error of judgment, not criminal negligence. There was no evidence of gross or rash negligence required for criminal liability under Section 304A IPC. Therefore, continuing the trial against her was unjustified.

Key Holdings:

- **Gross Negligence is Essential:** Criminal prosecution of a medical professional requires proof of gross negligence or recklessness. Mere inadvertence, an error of judgment, or an unsuccessful outcome does not attract criminal liability.
- **Error of Judgment is Not a Crime:** The Court observed that, at best, the allegations suggested an error of clinical judgment, which falls short of the threshold for criminal negligence.
- **Parity Among Co-Accused:** Since another treating doctor facing substantially similar allegations had already been discharged, there was no justification for continuing prosecution against Dr. Ingole alone.
- **Jacob Mathew Principles Reaffirmed:** The Court reiterated that the principles laid down in Jacob Mathew v. State of Punjab (2005) continue to govern criminal prosecutions against doctors. Criminal liability arises only

when the conduct demonstrates a very high degree of negligence amounting to recklessness.

- **Protection Against Frivolous Prosecution:** The judgment emphasised that criminal law should not be invoked merely because treatment was unsuccessful or the patient died, as such prosecutions discourage the medical profession and promote defensive medicine.

Compensation / Outcome

The Supreme Court dealt with the question of criminal liability of a doctor accused of causing death by negligence under Section 304A of the Indian Penal Code. The Court held that the allegations against Dr. Sou Jayshree Ujwal Ingole did not disclose the level of gross or reckless negligence required for criminal prosecution. It quashed the criminal proceedings, reiterating that a medical professional cannot be prosecuted merely because a patient suffered an adverse outcome unless there is clear evidence of a high degree of negligence.

Significance & Impact:

Dr. Sou Jayshree Ujwal Ingole v. State of Maharashtra & Anr. reaffirmed the distinction between civil medical negligence and criminal medical negligence. The judgment emphasised that criminal law should be invoked against doctors only in cases of gross negligence or recklessness, not for ordinary errors of judgment or unsuccessful treatment. It strengthened the safeguards laid down in *Jacob Mathew v. State of Punjab* and protected medical professionals from unwarranted criminal proceedings while preserving remedies for genuine cases of negligence.

SIGNIFICANCE AND PRECEDENTIAL VALUE

- This judgment reaffirms the distinction between civil negligence and criminal negligence in medical practice.
- It reinforces the principle that criminal prosecution of doctors is warranted only where there is evidence of gross negligence and not for every adverse medical outcome.
- The decision strengthens the protective framework established in Jacob Mathew v. State of Punjab, ensuring that doctors are not subjected to criminal trials for bona fide errors of judgment or complications inherent in medical treatment.

MEDLEX360 PRACTICE PEARLS	
What went wrong?	Criminal proceedings were initiated despite the absence of evidence demonstrating gross negligence. The allegations, even if accepted, reflected at most an error of clinical judgment rather than recklessness amounting to a criminal offence.
Risk Management Takeaways	• Maintain complete and contemporaneous medical records • Clearly document clinical findings and the rationale for treatment decisions • Record consultations with specialists and multidisciplinary discussions • Ensure prompt referral where clinically indicated • Obtain informed consent after discussing foreseeable risks and limitations of treatment

MEDLEX360 PRACTICE PEARLS	
	• Preserve all treatment records for potential medico-legal scrutiny.
Documentation Checklist	• Complete inpatient treatment records • Progress notes • Investigation reports • Consultation and referral records • Nursing records • Consent forms • Discharge summary

Criminal liability attaches only to grossly negligent or reckless medical conduct.

Glossary of Legal Terms and Maxims

A sound understanding of medico-legal terminology is essential for both healthcare professionals and young lawyers navigating medical negligence and healthcare litigation.

For doctors, familiarity with these concepts promotes legally compliant clinical practice, strengthens documentation, and supports informed decision-making.

For lawyers, these terms provide the foundation for analysing medical disputes, evaluating evidence, and understanding the legal principles that govern professional liability.

This glossary serves as a quick reference to the key legal concepts and Latin maxims most frequently encountered in Indian medico-legal practice.

Term / Maxim	Meaning / Relevance
Act of Omission	Failure to do something that a reasonably competent doctor ought to have done (e.g., failure to monitor, investigate, refer, or obtain consent).
Act of Commission	Performing an act improperly or doing something that should not have been done (e.g., operating on the wrong site or administering the wrong drug).

Term / Maxim	Meaning / Relevance
Adverse Event	An undesirable outcome during treatment, which may or may not result from negligence.
Assault	Intentional act creating apprehension of unlawful physical contact; in healthcare, treatment without valid consent may constitute assault.
Battery	Intentional physical contact without lawful consent. Performing a procedure without consent may amount to battery.
Bolam Test	A doctor is not negligent if the treatment is in accordance with a practice accepted as proper by a responsible body of medical professionals skilled in that field.
Bolitho Test	Courts may reject a body of medical opinion if it is not logical, reasonable, or defensible. Supplements the Bolam Test.
Burden of Proof	Obligation to prove a claim. In medical negligence, the complainant generally bears this burden unless shifted by law or circumstances.
Cause of Action	The facts giving a person the legal right to seek relief before a court or tribunal.

Term / Maxim	Meaning / Relevance
Civil Negligence	Breach of a duty of care causing harm, resulting in liability to pay compensation.
Contributory Negligence	When the patient's own conduct contributes to the injury or damage suffered.
Criminal Negligence	Gross or reckless negligence attracting criminal liability, generally requiring a very high degree of carelessness.
Damages	Monetary compensation awarded for injury, loss, disability, or death caused by negligence.
Deficiency in Service	Under consumer law, any fault, imperfection, shortcoming, or inadequacy in the quality or manner of healthcare services.
Duty of Care	The legal obligation of healthcare professionals to provide treatment consistent with the accepted standard of care.
Expert Evidence	Opinion given by a qualified medical expert to assist the court in understanding technical medical issues.

Term / Maxim	Meaning / Relevance
Foreseeability	Whether a reasonably competent doctor could have anticipated the risk of harm.
Good Faith	Honest action taken with due care and attention, often relevant under statutory protections for healthcare professionals.
Gross Negligence	A very serious departure from accepted standards of care showing reckless disregard for patient safety.
Informed Consent	Consent given after the patient has been adequately informed about the nature, risks, benefits, alternatives, and consequences of a procedure.
Medical Negligence	Failure to exercise the degree of skill and care expected of a reasonably competent medical professional, resulting in harm.
Mens Rea	"Guilty mind." The mental element required for many criminal offences. Usually absent in ordinary civil negligence.
No-Fault Compensation	Compensation awarded without requiring proof of negligence, usually under statutory or welfare schemes.

Term / Maxim	Meaning / Relevance
Preponderance of Probabilities	Standard of proof in civil cases; the claim is more likely true than not.
Proof Beyond Reasonable Doubt	Standard of proof in criminal cases requiring a much higher level of certainty.
Professional Misconduct	Conduct violating ethical or professional standards, attracting disciplinary action by medical regulatory authorities.
Proximate Cause	The direct and legally recognised cause of injury.
Reasonable Care	The level of care expected from an ordinarily competent practitioner in similar circumstances.
Res Ipsa Loquitur	*"The thing speaks for itself."* The occurrence itself may permit an inference of negligence where the event ordinarily would not happen without negligence and the instrumentality was under the defendant's control.
Res Judicata	*"A matter already adjudicated."* A dispute finally decided by a competent court cannot ordinarily be litigated again between the same parties.

Term / Maxim	Meaning / Relevance
Standard of Care	The degree of skill, diligence, and competence expected from a reasonably skilled healthcare professional in similar circumstances.
Strict Liability	Liability imposed without proof of negligence in limited situations prescribed by law.
Tort	A civil wrong, other than breach of contract, for which the law provides a remedy, usually compensation.
Vicarious Liability	Liability of a hospital or employer for the negligent acts or omissions of its employees or agents committed during the course of employment.
Volenti Non Fit Injuria	*"To a willing person, no injury is done."* A person who voluntarily accepts a known risk generally cannot later complain of harm arising solely from that accepted risk.

Important Legal Maxims in Medico-Legal Practice

Maxim	Meaning / Application
Actori Incumbit Onus Probandi	*The burden of proof lies on the plaintiff.* The complainant generally must establish negligence.
Audi Alteram Partem	*Hear the other side.* A fundamental principle of natural justice requiring both parties to be given an opportunity to be heard.
Delegatus Non Potest Delegare	*A delegate cannot further delegate.* Relevant where duties entrusted to a professional cannot be improperly delegated.
Ignorantia Juris Non Excusat	*Ignorance of the law is no excuse.* Healthcare professionals are expected to know the legal obligations governing their practice.
Novus Actus Interveniens	*A new intervening act.* An independent event that breaks the chain of causation between the original act and the injury.
Primum Non Nocere	*First, do no harm.* An ethical principle emphasizing patient safety, though not an independent legal rule.

Maxim	Meaning / Application
Qui Facit Per Alium Facit Per Se	*He who acts through another acts himself.* Forms the basis of vicarious liability of hospitals for acts of their staff.
Res Ipsa Loquitur	*The thing speaks for itself.* Applied in obvious negligence cases such as retained surgical sponges or wrong blood transfusions.
Salus Populi Suprema Lex	*The welfare of the people is the supreme law.* Supports public health measures and healthcare regulation.
Ubi Jus Ibi Remedium	*Where there is a right, there is a remedy.* A patient whose legal rights are violated is entitled to seek an appropriate legal remedy.

Ten Medico-Legal Rules

Every doctor should follow the ten universal medico-legal rules encapsulated in this chapter. The cases discussed throughout this book arise from different specialties, different hospitals, different circumstances, and different periods of time. Yet, when examined closely, most medico-legal disputes originate from a surprisingly small number of recurring mistakes.

Rarely does litigation arise solely because of a poor outcome. More often, disputes emerge from inadequate communication, incomplete documentation, unclear consent, delayed escalation, or a breakdown of trust between the healthcare team and the patient.

The principles outlined below are not derived from any single judgment. Rather, they represent the common lessons that emerge repeatedly from Indian medico-legal jurisprudence.

Whether one practices in a tertiary care hospital, a small clinic, an emergency department, or a rural health centre, these rules remain universally applicable.

Rule 1: Document Everything

If it is not documented, it may be difficult to prove that it happened.

Medical records form the foundation of a doctor's legal defence. Courts, consumer fora, medical councils, and expert committees rely heavily on contemporaneous documentation when evaluating allegations of negligence.

Good documentation demonstrates clinical reasoning, decision-making, patient communication, informed consent, and continuity of care.

Poor documentation creates uncertainty, and uncertainty often works against the healthcare provider.

Key Points

- Write legibly and contemporaneously.
- Record clinical findings accurately.
- Document differential diagnoses.
- Record treatment decisions and reasons.
- Note patient counselling discussions.
- Maintain discharge summaries carefully.

Remember

- The strongest witness in any medico-legal case is often the medical record

Rule 2: Obtain Meaningful Informed Consent

Consent is not a signature.

The Supreme Court in Samira Kohli emphasised that patients have the right to make informed decisions regarding their treatment. Consent obtained without adequate information is neither ethically nor legally sufficient.

Patients should understand:

- The diagnosis.
- The proposed treatment.
- Material risks.
- Expected benefits.
- Available alternatives.
- Consequences of refusal.

Key Points

- Use procedure-specific consent forms.
- Explain significant risks honestly.
- Encourage questions.
- Document the discussion.
- Obtain fresh consent when circumstances change.

Remember

- A signed form proves a signature. Good documentation proves informed consent.

Rule 3: Communicate Clearly and Frequently

Many medico-legal disputes begin as communication failures.

Patients and families are often willing to accept complications when they understand what happened, why it happened, and what is being done to address it.

Uncertainty, silence, and inconsistent explanations frequently generate mistrust.

Key Points

- Provide realistic expectations.
- Discuss complications promptly.
- Communicate treatment plans clearly.
- Maintain consistency among treating teams.
- Record important discussions.

Remember

- Patients are more likely to forgive complications than poor communication.

Rule 4: Never Alter Medical Records

Nothing damages professional credibility more quickly than tampering with records.

Courts view alterations, overwriting, missing entries, and retrospective changes with extreme suspicion.

If a correction is necessary:

- Strike through the incorrect entry.
- Make a corrected entry.
- Record the date and time.
- Authenticate the correction.

Key Points

- Never erase original entries.
- Never create records retrospectively.
- Preserve electronic audit trails.
- Maintain integrity of all documents.

Remember

- A complication may be defensible. Altered records rarely are.

Rule 5: Treat Emergencies First

The duty to provide emergency medical care is one of the clearest obligations recognised by Indian courts.

Cases such as Parmanand Katara and Pravat Kumar Mukherjee establish that preservation of life takes precedence over procedural and financial considerations.

Key Points

- Stabilize the patient immediately.
- Do not delay treatment due to payment issues.
- Arrange timely referral when necessary.
- Document emergency interventions.

Remember

- In an emergency, treatment comes first and paperwork follows.

Rule 6: Respect Patient Confidentiality

Confidentiality is a cornerstone of medical practice. Patients disclose deeply personal information because they trust that it will remain protected. However, as seen in Mr. X v. Hospital Z, confidentiality is not absolute. Limited disclosure may sometimes be justified to prevent serious harm or comply with legal obligations.

Key Points

- Share information on a need-to-know basis.
- Obtain consent where appropriate.
- Understand statutory reporting obligations.
- Document reasons for disclosure.

Remember

•Confidentiality is the rule. Disclosure is the exception.

Rule 7: Know Your Limits and Escalate Early

Medicine is increasingly complex.

No doctor is expected to know everything. Courts generally appreciate timely referral and multidisciplinary management.

Delays in seeking specialist assistance often attract greater criticism than the original diagnostic challenge.

Key Points

- Refer appropriately.
- Seek second opinions.
- Escalate deteriorating patients promptly.
- Document consultations and referrals.

Remember

•Seeking help is a sign of professionalism, not weakness.

Rule 8: Follow Accepted Standards of Care

The law does not demand perfection.

It requires that a doctor act in accordance with standards accepted by a responsible body of medical professionals.

Courts generally avoid substituting their judgment for clinical expertise. However, departures from accepted standards require justification.

Key Points

- Follow evidence-based practices.
- Adhere to institutional protocols.
- Remain updated with current guidelines.
- Document reasons for deviations when necessary.

Remember

- A reasonable decision is defensible even when the outcome is unfavorable.

Rule 9: Preserve Records and Evidence

A medico-legal case may arise years after treatment.

Records that seem routine today may become critical evidence in future proceedings.

The inability to produce records often creates adverse inferences against the healthcare provider.

Key Points

- Follow statutory retention requirements.
- Preserve investigation reports.
- Maintain imaging records.
- Secure electronic backups.
- Retain consent documentation.

Remember

•Records cannot defend you if they no longer exist.

Rule 10: Practice Ethical Medicine Every Day

Ethics and law are closely connected.

Most medico-legal disputes involve conduct that is not only legally problematic but also ethically questionable.

Honesty, transparency, respect, compassion, and professionalism remain the most reliable safeguards against litigation.

Key Points

- Place patient welfare first.
- Be truthful about complications.
- Avoid conflicts of interest.
- Respect patient autonomy.
- Maintain professional boundaries.

Remember

•Good ethics is often the best medico-legal defence.

MEDLEX360 MASTER CHECKLIST

Before concluding any patient encounter, ask yourself:

- ☐ Have I documented my findings?
- ☐ Have I obtained and recorded informed consent?
- ☐ Have I communicated clearly with the patient or family?
- ☐ Have I documented important discussions?
- ☐ Have I preserved confidentiality?
- ☐ Have I followed accepted standards of care?
- ☐ Have I sought help where necessary?
- ☐ Have I maintained accurate records?
- ☐ Have I acted in the patient's best interests?
- ☐ Would my documentation allow another doctor or a court to understand exactly what happened?

Final Thought

The purpose of medico-legal awareness is not to encourage defensive medicine. The objective is to promote safe, ethical, transparent, and patient-centred healthcare.

Most legal disputes can be prevented long before they reach a courtroom. The principles discussed throughout this book - and summarized in this chapter - provide a practical framework for reducing risk while improving patient care.

Every landmark judgment in this book teaches a legal lesson. Together, they teach a professional one: good medicine, good communication, and good documentation remain the strongest medico-legal safeguards available to every doctor.

www.ingramcontent.com/pod-product-compliance
Lightning Source LLC
LaVergne TN
LVHW070451220926
848482LV00045B/393
9798905847509